SECOND EDITION

Designing
PROFESSIONAL
DEVELOPMENT
for Change

To the memory of Asa Hilliard: friend, colleague, and mentor.

In my last visit with Asa in the spring of 2007, we discussed the state of professional development, especially as it applied to children of color and poverty. A major part of Asa's life was dedicated to the preparation of teachers of these children.

In the early 1990s, he urged me to become involved with Reuven Feurestein's theory and practices. Over the years, Asa actively supported my work disseminating Feuerstein's programs. At that last meeting, we began plans for a large research project with an urban school district that would make a systemic use of Feuerstein's Instrumental Enrichment.

During our discussion, a former student of Asa's greeted him and made a request. He wanted Asa to sign on as an advisor to a basic skills reading research project for a publisher. Asa declined the lucrative offer. Afterwards, he said to me, "Do you know why I did that? It is not about the money. It is about what I want to spend my time doing now. Projects to measure minute reading skills are a dime a dozen. If you make little pieces small enough, you can prove anything. I want to spend my time making a difference. For that, I want to work on research that measures substantive efforts that make a big difference in children's lives. Feuerstein's programs give that. Measuring how many phonics sounds a child recalls never will."

Asa's distinction between minutia and substance was pure and wonderful Asa. This is why the field of professional development will miss him. This is why I am thankful for the time I had to learn from his wisdom. This is why I will miss him.

—Jim Bellanca

SECOND EDITION

Designing
PROFESSIONAL
DEVELOPMENT
for Change

A Guide for
Improving
Classroom
Instruction

JAMES BELLANCA

CORWIN PRESS
A SAGE Company

For information:

Corwin Press
A SAGE Company
2455 Teller Road
Thousand Oaks, California 91320
www.corwinpress.com

SAGE India Pvt. Ltd.
B 1/I 1 Mohan Cooperative
   Industrial Area
Mathura Road, New Delhi
India 110 044

SAGE Ltd.
1 Oliver's Yard
55 City Road
London EC1Y 1SP
United Kingdom

SAGE Asia-Pacific Pte. Ltd.
33 Pekin Street #02-01
Far East Square
Singapore 048763

Printed in the United States of America.

Library of Congress Cataloging-in-Publication Data

Bellanca, James A., 1937-
Designing professional development for change: A guide for improving classroom instruction / James Bellanca.—2nd ed.
     p. cm.

Includes bibliographical references.
ISBN 978-1-4129-6545-3 (cloth)
ISBN 978-1-4129-6546-0 (pbk.)
    1. Teachers—In-service training—Planning. 2. Educational change. 3. Transfer of training. I. Title.

LB1731.B445 2009
370.71'5'—dc22   2008028869

This book is printed on acid-free paper.

08   09   10   11   12   10   9   8   7   6   5   4   3   2   1

Acquisitions Editor:	Cathy Hernandez
Associate Editor:	Desirée Enayati
Production Editor:	Eric Garner
Copy Editor:	Gretchen Treadwell
Typesetter:	C&M Digitals (P) Ltd.
Proofreader:	Charlotte J. Waisner
Cover Designer:	Scott Van Atta

Contents

Preface to the Second Edition

Welcome to this new and substantially updated revision of *Professional Development for Change*. Since the publication of the original version in 1995, much has happened within the field—new practices, new research, new ideas, and new foci.

In the 1960s, when I first became a developer of teachers, the inservice day was the primary model of professional development. With the opportunity to work with Madeline Hunter, Roger and David Johnson, Art Costa, Larry Chase, Bernice McCarthy, Tom McGreal, and others who were stepping forward with week-long workshops, I began my studies of what worked. Over the years, this lead to collaborations with Ron Brandt, Robin Fogarty, Howard Gardner, and others who influenced my thoughts on how the workshop model might best help teachers bring their new learning to the classroom. The work of Bruce Joyce and Beverly Showers, as well as that of Art Costa and Bob Garmston with their seminal research on the role of coaching, lead to studies of learning transfer based on the work of David Perkins and his associates.

Throughout the 1980s, professional developers relied on the workshop as the principle practice. Even today, in spite of efforts by the National Staff Development Council (NSDC) to move professional developers from their reliance on the workshop format to an emphasis on learning communities, the workshop remains the dominant medium for professional development. In fact, there are a plethora of districts and many educational organizations, including NSDC, that adhere to the one-shot workshop in many of their conferences.

In the early 1990s, Beau Fly Jones and Barbara Preseissan from the National Labs introduced me to Reuven Feuerstein. Asa Hilliard, a long-time advocate of Feuerstein's work applied to children of poverty and color, seconded the idea that I become involved with disseminating Reuven's work. Together, we planned the first Teaching for Intelligence Conference in Taunton, Massachusetts. Asa keynoted that conference and the subsequent Teaching for Intelligence conferences, which featured the school districts using Feuerstein's work.

As recently as the spring of 2007, Asa and I were continuing our get-togethers to discuss how to best advance Reuven's core ideas into American schools. At that meeting, we were planning how Asa could lead a research project on what he called "the most substantive program I know for changing children's minds so that they could learn better." Sadly, not long after, I received word of Asa's untimely and tragic death.

Over the years, I have studied and used Feuestein's principles of learning to undergird my understanding of how cognition impacts the teaching and learning for not only children, but also for adults. His theory of the mediated learning experience, reinforced by hundreds of research and evaluation studies, aligns tightly with the "shepherding" concepts of Perkins, Barell, and Fogarty. Both "mediated" learning and "shepherded" transfer of learning encourage the construction of new understandings facilitated by the interventions of a well-prepared teacher who has the intention of teaching for transfer.

In this scenario, learning is not left to chance. Without the mediation or shepherding, many adult learners can easily miss much of the depth of meaning and the reach of knowledge transfer. They can stay stuck in the "information is enough" mode of learning that they mastered in college and become mired in the swamp of immediate results, as opposed to finding ways to make instruction soar to the heights. With a Bo-Peep "mediator" who skillfully bridges new concepts into new dimensions of knowing, adult learners more quickly and more deeply make new cognitive connections across the curriculum. As pressed for time as teachers are, shepherded mediation is an alternative that can't be overlooked if transfer is the goal. While reaching for the transfer goal, teachers not only raise students' test scores, but they enable their students to learn for a lifetime.

In the professional work that my colleagues and I do today, we attempt to make use of what we have learned through successful practices and continued intentional transfer of our own new learning into the schools with which we work. The new content in this edition reflects what we have learned, yet does not abandon practices that have continued to help teachers help children.

Professional development for educators continues to evolve as a science. As new instructional practices are validated by research, they become more accepted. Some practices are replaced. Others forgotten. However, it is important for professional developers in search of sustainable improvements to remember that such improvements are first and foremost for the students, not the teachers. Improvement of teacher performance is a means to an end, not the end itself.

WHAT IS NEW IN THIS EDITION

With these principles in mind, some of the new concepts I have introduced into this book include:

1. A focus on the roles of the site-based professional developer as a champion for change in a learning community that is student-centered.

2. A focus on the assessment of a school's low-performing students' learning needs as the starting point for creating a sustainable long-term program to improve academic achievement for all.

3. A connection among those theories and practices of adult learning that result in the most effective learning transfer into classroom practice.

4. A framework for guiding professional developers through three stages of implementation that ensures the strongest sustainability.

5. An emphasis on how to best facilitate teachers' transference of new understandings gathered from multiple sources of information that will best improve achievement by all students at a school site.

6. The importance of mediated learning experiences through skillful coaching of adult learners as they gather information, make sense of its value for their students, and implement new approaches.

7. An explicit alignment of transfer theory and practice with the goal of program sustainability.

This book is a primer. Like the start of a master garden, this primer highlights the "the bones" of the garden of learning. The bones are those structures set in place to guide where various plants will go in the garden's completed plan. In this analogy, the gardener is the site-based professional developer, be that person the school's administrator, a professional development specialist, or a team of teachers assigned the responsibility. The professional developer, like the master gardener, wears many hats.

After a professional developer at the school site has designed the garden with its key elements marked—the trees, the bushes, the flower beds—she will consult other resources—the flower catalogs and local garden shops—to learn about the various perennials and annuals that will best fit in the plan. After professional developers have planted their choices, they will add the organic fertilizer, water, and other elements of love and care, which will turn their seedlings into the beautiful garden they can till and enjoy for many, many years.

Acknowledgments

I want to thank those persons who contributed to this new edition:

- Donna Ramirez for her formatting and "clean up"
- Kate Bellanca for her feedback and figure designs
- Dave Stockman for his cartoon sketches.

Thanks all.

PUBLISHER'S ACKNOWLEDGMENTS

Corwin Press gratefully acknowledges the contributions of the following individuals:

Nancy A. Carey, Coordinator
  of Professional Development
Maryland State Department of Education
Baltimore, MD

Linda C. Diaz, Program Specialist for
  Professional Development
Monroe County School District
Key West, FL

David Freitas, Professor
Indiana University South Bend
South Bend, IN

Nora G. Friedman, Principal
South Grove Elementary School
Syosset, NY

Nancy Kellogg, Science Education Consultant
Boulder, CO

About the Author

 **James Bellanca.** After twelve years as an award-winning teacher, Jim's career shifted when he was asked to lead teams of teachers in finding better ways to enrich students' learning experiences. During the next ten years, he developed two innovative alternative school programs, a Regional Special Education Professional Development Program and a Regional Service Center for Professional Development. In 1982, he founded SkyLight Publishing and Professional Development, Inc. and through this company, he championed the introduction of best instructional practices. These include cooperative learning, asking questions, multiple intelligences, and cognitive instruction. Collaborating with Madeline Hunter, Roger and David Johnson, Art Costa, Howard Gardner, Reuven Feuerstein, Ron Brandt, Robin Fogarty, Carolyn Chapman and other leaders in the professional development arena, Jim developed pioneering publications and programs to provide teachers with the most practical ways to use these strategies. At the same time, he authored and coauthored more than two-dozen books that introduced the intensive use of instructional strategies for improving achievement. Among his publications are *What Is It About Me That You Can't Teach?*, *Graphic Organizers*, *Multiple Assessments for Multiple Intelligences*, *BluePrints for Achievement in the Cooperative Classroom*, and the preceding edition of *Professional Development for Change*.

Why Change?

Old ideas and processes must be tossed aside so that new ones can be learned. Often, getting rid of the old idea is just as difficult as learning the new ones.

—Kurt Lewin

"You've been teaching here for five years... It is time for review. You're at a key juncture. Because of your superior teaching, I am going to recommend your advancement to Merit Level II. However, before I do that, I want us to review your file and determine how much you have improved over these last five years."

Those were the words of my department chair. When I was first hired to teach English at New Trier East, Mary Ida was a colleague. Now, she was my boss. In the review that followed, we had weekly conversations. The process she used, dictated by our teacher's union contract but colored by her rigor, reviewed the annual observations of my classroom work, my committee work, and other parts of my school life. Mary Ida, being the stickler she was, focused our dialogues on what I was doing to change for the better.

(Continued)

(Continued)

In the following years, while I had many other "reviews," none impacted my teaching so deeply as that first review. "Teaching," she taught me, "is about change. If you are not striving to change the minds and hearts of your students, you are not teaching well. To have any significant impact on what and how students learn, it is essential that you yourself change for the better. If you don't, they won't."

Mary Ida's thoughts stayed with me in the years that followed. They influenced my own quest to improve my teaching so that my students could improve their learning. "Change is," as Mary Ida would repeat, "a lifelong quest that begins with each teacher's inherent drive to teach each student as well as possible."

DOES DEVELOPMENT ALWAYS MEAN CHANGE?

At first glance, it may seem redundant to talk about professional development and change in the same breath. Is it not obvious that any act labeled "development" is about change? Is it not understood that all teachers participate in professional development so that they can change for the better?

The answer to these questions is "no" and "yes." First, consider the "no" side. If social studies teachers take a graduate course to better understand the causes of the Revolutionary War, they end their study with a test of knowledge. The final exam finishes the study. The notes are packed away and the course credits recorded in the personnel office. Individuals can then decide if they will use the new knowledge in their classes. They may adjust a specific unit or integrate some new acquired facts in a lesson. Or, they may simply store the knowledge away for another day, take their earned credits or points, and teach the original course syllabus without any change. Is new knowledge acquired? Yes. Transfer to the classroom? No. In the context of professional development *for change*, there is no *change* when teachers acquire new material, but elect not to transfer it into the courses they teach.

The answer turns to a "yes" on both sides when teachers transform new knowledge and skills gained from a course, workshop, or learning project into classroom lessons or materials. To assist this transformation, teachers' professional development must require much more than the acquisition of new knowledge. Gathering new knowledge or developing new skills are only the first elements of any learning experience that will contribute to the transfer of what the teachers actually learn in order for their students to understand well what they are learning.

Is Information Enough?

For centuries, educators have considered learning as a mere information transfer activity. One person with more knowledge passes it on to others with less knowledge. The master carpenter passes his skills to the apprentice. The university scholar fills the minds of his students.

Even today, the medieval "pass-it-on" model dominates most academic disciplines. The professor researcher spends three decades in the Antarctica studying the role of krill in the food chain. He returns to the university once a year to lecture undergraduates in Marine Biology 101. The professor of education surveys the history of education for her graduate students. She passes important names and movements that have impacted American education into their notebooks and exam papers. From all appearances, "the sit and git" model, which psychologist Carl Rogers lampooned almost a half century ago as "process akin to pouring a gallon of water into an empty jug," thrives on teacher talk.

So deeply ingrained is this "tell us the information" phenomenon that students demand it even in a discipline such as mathematics. "My students get angry when I don't lecture on the problems that are examples of a concept I am teaching.

They want to write the solution down step-by-step. Here I am with these doctoral candidates and they still just want the facts," lamented a professor of theoretical mathematics.

In spite of what Marzano and colleagues' (2001) meta-analysis of "what works" in the classroom and what adult learning researchers say, the pour it in syndrome also thrives in professional development workshops, and in graduate courses as well. The main difference? It looks as if the number of days required to earn the credits is the only variable that distinguishes graduate course work from professional development workshops.

Wherever the professional development of teachers follows the centuries-old model of direct information transmission from "expert" to "novice," the most significant change is the amount of information in the individual's brain. Bruce Joyce and Beverly Showers, in their landmark study conducted in 1983, noted that less than 10 percent of the information transmitted via lecture alone had any impact on true learning in the classroom. They went so far as to report that the addition of a demonstration had no more effect than the lecture alone. Change still happened in the smallest percentages. However, when teachers were engaged by coaches, especially their peers, in carefully structured investigations—based on peer observation, feedback, and revision of lesson plans that *used* the original information—almost 90 percent of the participants made significant changes in how and what they taught. Thus, in the Joyce and Shower's study, a change in practice happens when other factors are added that facilitate the transmission of passive information into instructional action.

MOVING TOWARD PURPOSEFUL CHANGE

How does a significant change *process* play out in professional development? In its simplest and often most powerful form, change works best as a collegial effort that focuses the learners on how they will actually improve their instructions by transferring static information into action. This change does

"That's about enough for today."

not rely on the assumption that information is enough. It anticipates that change occurs via a purposeful, collaborative process that begins with the sharing of new information, new ideas, new skills or new beliefs, but continues on.

Consider, for example, six high school teachers who were faced with two dilemmas: obtaining their recertification and using new knowledge. First, it was time for their recertification requirement to end. All needed at least three credits. Second, they all taught American history. In the districts' new U.S. history syllabus, they were required to cover the Vietnam War, yet none had ever completed course work that included this conflict. After meeting with the assistant principal, who was also in charge of professional development, the teachers presented a plan based on the teacher-contract for a 45-hour course titled "The Vietnam War: Causes and Results."

The assistant principal rejected their proposal. He turned down the syllabus because it called for forty-five hours of seatwork. He suggested the teachers use the 75-hour prospectus that the union had recently agreed to as an alternative approach to recertification. He explained what it would entail: two research papers by each of the six; each paper had to cover a different aspect of the war and had to come from different resources, one of which could be the course's professor. Each paper would earn the equivalent of fifteen hours of seat time. After analyzing and discussing each other's work, they would create a one-week syllabus for their American history classes.

All would teach the syllabus and all would observe at least two of their peers in action. Following the observations, they would share what they had seen and heard and discuss what each might do differently. Next, all would write papers summarizing what they had learned and how they felt the students would gain. Finally, they would share these papers.

These teachers were asked to experience professional development as both a change process and a result. Not only would they acquire new information and deepen their understanding of the causes of war, they would analyze the information to see how it best fit into their courses, plan their course modifications, and assess the impact of the changes on themselves and their students. Thus, they experienced a learning process that required them to use what they learned. Although not using "pure" Joyce and Showers, these six teachers made valid transfer of the elements needed to move from a course that emphasized information gathering to a professional development model that helped them put the information into classroom practice and transform their teaching efforts. And, they earned their hours!

Intentional Transfer Is a Must

Professional development is a significant change process when the transfer of learning from abstract information to classroom practice is intentional. Such a change does not occur simply because teachers acquire new information, no matter what the means is by which they gather it. The change occurs when teachers have the support systems that carry them through the phases of learning in which they make sense of that information and then integrate their new understandings into classroom lessons.

Summary Points

1. Professional development guides teachers through a change process that should culminate in a transfer of learning. Neither the change nor the transfer will be easy.

2. Transfer of learning requires a support system provided to best ensure that new ideas become new actions.

3. During the transfer process, teachers' learning experiences pass through three phases: information gathering, making sense of new concepts, and integrating new understandings into classroom practice.

A Paradigm Shift

When I first suggested to the teachers to not worry about what they wanted, but instead focus on student needs, they were very skeptical. After they saw the first year results, they couldn't wait to continue.

—Sandi Garr
Glenfair Elementary School
Portland, Oregon

The Three Bears at the North Pole

"We've been sitting on this piece of ice for a long time," said Elsie to her mother.

"I know, dear," responded the mother polar bear. "But it's too cold to swim."

"Does this happen every year? I thought Daddy said the ice never melts around here," said the little bear.

"That is the way it was in the good old days. But in the last few years, the ice has melted more and more."

"Does that mean that nice little girl won't be coming for breakfast?" asked the little, baby bear. "It's fun when she comes and sleeps in my bed and I get to wake her up in the morning."

"I don't think so," replied the mother bear. "Since she broke the ice in front of the door last year, we haven't seen her."

"Oh, look. I see father bear over there on that other ice flow. He's caught some fish. Do you think he'll swim over? "

"I told you, it's too cold. Polar bears hate to swim and your father is set in his ways."

"But if he doesn't swim over, we won't get our dinner," cried the baby bear.

"Out of the mouth of babes," sighed mother bear. "If only your father could change as easily as the weather."

"What are we going to do? I am so-o-o hungry."

A WIN-WIN START

In the early days of inservice, teachers often galloped to a county or state fair ground for inspiration. Hundreds gathered to hear the superintendent tell them "what's new." By the 1960s, inservice was supplemented with opportunities for teachers to perfect the "art of teaching" with graduate course work and staff development activities. Personal development was the password.

In the next thirty years, research on "best instructional" practices and programs transformed the quest for improvement from an individual, personal responsibility to a schoolwide requirement (see Figure 2.1). Accountability for improving student performance, especially among children of poverty, minority groups, English language learners, and students with special needs, became the bye-word that called for applications of research-based practices in the classroom. With the new emphasis on scientifically based research and schoolwide accountability came the need for a new paradigm of professional development. The new paradigm

Figure 2.1   A Paradigm Shift in Continuing Education of
Teachers

Pre-1990		Post-1990
Art	→	Science
Personal Development	→	Professional Development
Acquiring Knowledge	→	Using Knowledge
Individual Growth	→	Schoolwide Accountability

could not assume that information was sufficient to bring the needed changes.

To avoid the frustrations and the resistance that inevitably emerge when teachers are required to change what or how they teach—changes that they often perceive as shallow, whimsical, nonsensical, unreasonable or "that's just plain stupid"—professional developers can experience greater success if they start the change process with a focused substantive needs assessment on the learning challenges which face their students, as opposed to the personal "wants" of the teachers.

In this age of accountability, teachers do not want or need to hear frivolous requests for shallow inservice activities such as "make and take" workshops or "show and tell" from a consultant who dances and sings. In response to such events, the best that they can mutter is "this too will pass." They know how short their actual teaching time is already. Distractions are numerous. Every school day is packed with unpredictable interruptions and calamities. Time allotted for serious instruction is crammed with increasing additional mandates. The number of students with second language backgrounds, difficult socioeconomic conditions, and special needs adds additional challenges. "Just let me teach" is often the teachers' plea. "Don't fix me up."

To avoid the swamp of teacher resistance created by quick-fix inservice programs, effective professional developers know that their best possibility for success is a highly focused learning experience that will lighten the teachers' load. Nothing satisfies this need more quickly than professional learning experiences that increase chances of success with students' learning. Such is the win-win nature of a well-prepared professional development needs assessment: a dual focus on students' deepest learning needs and the teachers' desire for productive and useful professional learning experiences that improve student learning.

STUDENT LEARNING NEEDS: THE FIRST PRIORITY

Constructing professional learning experiences that achieve the goal of strengthening student learning, especially the learning of those students who have struggled continuously over many years, is akin to a Titanic-sinking, iceberg-sized challenge.

Experienced educators understand that such experiences are best begun with a substantive needs assessment that uncovers the deep issues that have hampered students' success. When teachers' professional development focuses on student learning needs, the results of the needs assessment not only communicate that the coming professional learning experiences are serious and substantive, but also help structure the entire program toward an end that produces measurable results that hold significant meaning for the teachers.

THE VALUE OF STUDENT LEARNING-CENTERED ASSESSMENTS

A student learning-centered needs assessment seeks to discover what is most necessary in making each child be as successful as possible in the school's academic program. Such an assessment allows for the assessors to seek out what the students must master in a required standards-based curriculum. In addition, an assessment focused on student learning provides assessors with opportunities to dig deeper into the root causes of the students' difficulties. A deeper probe will take the assessment below the surface problems to identify undeveloped cognitive functions and negative belief systems, which have undermined the students' chances of becoming efficient learners.

WANTS: A SAND TRAP

Overall, the student learning perspective helps needs assessors and teachers to distinguish more sharply between "needs for learning" and "wants of teachers." "Wants" assessments are giant sand traps. Some of the most typical sand traps are teachers' espoused desires to learn about the latest educational fads, hear the hottest edutainers on the institute day circuit, or adapt to an administrator's pet project (or in some cases, pet peeve). Other sand traps in which "wants" are disguised as "needs" include no-cost workshops from the textbook publisher for those who want to save money, complaints from disgruntled staff members who want to continue teaching how they have been in spite of year after year of nonlearning by their students, and lists of superficial recertification topics for those who want their requirements most painlessly out of the way for the next five years.

"I didn't think sand traps counted."

THE SEVEN PRINCIPLES

Seven principles guide effective student-centered needs assessments. Use of these principles, based on the belief that teachers can bring about significant changes in students' learning potential as well as their test scores, are the foundation of the effective professional development programs that lead to significant changes in instruction.

1. Give *first* priority to identifying the learning needs of the students who are most in need of transforming their learning capabilities from deep failure to high success.

2. Identify the most serious and profound learning needs of the targeted students. Make special note of what is necessary to transforming their beliefs about their own learning capabilities from acceptance of failure to celebration of academic success.

3. Ascertain what is giving these students the most difficulty when learning the school's core curriculum.

4. Ensure that all professional staff practice a belief system that is committed to expanding the fullest learning potential of each child.

5. Identify the knowledge, skills, and belief changes that teachers will need to make in order to better facilitate the learning success of these students.

6. Establish a schoolwide learning environment intended to mediate those learning experiences that will be most powerful in changing the academic performance of these students.

7. Identify how teachers and administrators can collaborate to sustain the development of each student's cognitive development over time, so that all discover the far reaches of their learning potential.

CHANGING THE PARADIGM

Change is a scary word for many educators. It need not be. Studies have shown that most teachers are risk adverse. They want security, order, and a system in the work day. They don't want to be flooded with a random onslaught of new ideas, new students, new texts, or new fads every day.

Yet, certain types of change are necessary. Most necessary is the change that relieves struggling students of their burdens and opens up new learning opportunities for them. In the behaviorist paradigm that dominated in American schools at least until the 1950s, it was believed that only certain students had the capability to learn. College was not in the reach for many or even most. As the cognitive sciences developed, the voices of Piaget, Feuerstein, and Vygotsky sounded the first disparate challenges to the notion that intelligence is fixed. Not too long after, Gardener, Sternberg, Perkins, and others built their theories of learning on the understanding that the brain was structurally modifiable.

Fifty years ago, American educators laughed at Feuerstein's statement that all children could learn because all children's cognitive capabilities were modifiable. Today, as more recent educators read the new studies of the brain, many of these educators no longer deride the theory. They put it into practice in professional development and in the students' classrooms. The paradigm of change is shifting, albeit slowly.

NEW ROLES FOR A NEW PARADIGM

In the context of change theory and practice, the professional developer's job is diverse. Almost daily, the most effective professional development specialists challenge themselves to play several different roles. As they change the roles to meet the emerging needs of a school's effort to improve its teaching and learning, the most effective professional developers welcome knowing what it means to be a champion for change. The roles are many:

Cognitive Change Believer: Believes that the most resistant and struggling learners can change how they think, learn, and do. Applies this belief to the organization, its administrators, teachers, and all children.

Collaborator: Works with the administrative team to frame and accomplish goals that will transform the school into a community of learners striving to increase the learning capability and achievement results for every student.

Coordinator: Plans and manages learning activities that facilitate the site's goals for sustainable change.

Challenger: Leads the faculty in challenging assumptions about learning and teaching that discourage all teachers in a historically low performing school from determining a course bound for excellence.

Cognitive Mediator: Helps teachers sharpen and intensify their use of problem-solving skills for addressing students' learning needs.

Competency Developer: Focuses the teachers on developing their knowledge and skills on creating a belief system that spotlights the competency of all teachers to change student performance.

Climate Controller: Organizes and supports a learning environment that places student achievement through cognitive enrichment at the heart of all school activities.

Creator of Transfer: Uses the theory and practices of learning transfer to instigate the transformation of the school into a high-performance learning community.

Coach: Empowers teachers and administrators to apply innovative ideas for the benefits of all students, especially those who appear to be the most persistent low performers.

Constant Gardener: Designs a plan for giving teachers the best chance to change children's minds by changing their own teaching behavior.

Creative Problem Solver: Anticipates glitches in how the learning community works to achieve its goals for all, changing the learning patterns of all students. Enables teachers to find new ways to produce the desired results.

Summary Points

1. A school's professional development needs assessment is most helpful to all if it focuses on *student learning needs*.

2. Assessments based on teacher "wants" are a trap.

3. There are seven principles for guiding a student learning-centered needs assessment. The assessment of student needs for learning leads to the assessment of teacher needs for teaching.

4. Professional development for the science of teaching has priority over an individual's personal development as an artist/teacher.

5. In the new paradigm of change in professional development, the specialist's roles change as well.

Getting to the Heart of the Matter

A leaf that is destined to grow large is full of grooves and wrinkles at the start. Now if one has no patience and wants it smooth offhand like a willow leaf, there is trouble ahead.

—Goethe

"Martha has been my student for two years now. When she came from the fourth grade, her file showed she was one of the best students in the class. She never gave anyone trouble. She had memorized her multiplication tables. She could tell you about any sound in a word and she read fluently."

"What is the problem? Why didn't she pass the fifth grade?" asked the principal.

(Continued)

(Continued)

"Most importantly," Mr. Kent continued, "she doesn't understand a word she reads. What have you tried?"

"I have done everything I know how. I used Venn diagrams and webs, even a concept map. I had her keep a journal just to tell the story. She can't seem to put the story line in order," said the teacher. "If she can't understand, how can she get all the material in math and social studies she needs for the test?"

The principal took a moment to think. "Well, if it is not about Martha's basic skills and we can't get any results on the subject tests, I think we may have to look elsewhere. Either that or just pass her on."

"What more can we look at?" asked Mr. Kent.

"It looks like to me that you haven't yet found the heart of the matter. I think she needs some basic work with her thinking. If she can't compare or sequence, she needs help getting those skills in place. They are essential tools in every subject," said the principal. "I think we need to assess how she is thinking. Let's see where the cognitive deficiencies are and what we can do to help her get off this plateau."

IDENTIFYING STUDENTS WITH THE GREATEST LEARNING NEEDS

In the early days of professional development, when the county or state institute day held sway and teachers rode on horseback or buggy to a central site for their annual dose of inservice medicine, helping them develop their skills with a quick shot of motivation accompanied by a handful of skill-pills for mathematics or reading instruction was a practical approach. Subsequently, by the end of the twentieth century, the technology of professional development provided school leaders with options that made inservice days nearly obsolete.

As schools were held more accountable for the academic performance of all students, school leaders were forced to attend more closely to those students that often had been ignored, especially when it came to providing teachers with the knowledge and skills needed to meet this challenge.

To meet this challenge for serving all students, but especially those who experience the most difficulty learning the curriculum, and developing their learning potential, the first principle of needs assessment guidance entails identifying those students whose record of success is the weakest. It is likely that these are the same students who believe most strongly that learning is "not my thing" or for whom advanced study is an "impossible dream."

No School Is Immune

Every school has students whose tests results, classroom participation, and other behaviors say "I don't do school." Their academic performance is abysmal. Year in and year out, even the best teachers struggle to engage these students in successful learning experiences. No school is immune from the challenges these low performers provide.

Low performers are not the prerogative of schools with large populations of students who face poverty at home, students with English as a second language, minority students, or students with special needs. *All schools* enroll low performers. Some schools are more successful at hiding the students who may not be "college material." Others are more successful in persuading those who don't fit the academic mold to drop out quietly. Many schools simply ignore the existence of any low performers.

Improving Instruction: The Clearest Path

It is an often-stated truism that the most effective way to improve student achievement is to improve the quality of instruction. Unfortunately, this concept slips in practice.

Instead of selecting the improvement of instruction as the first priority for improving student performance, school leaders often select the easier, perhaps less contentious and certainly less-effective solutions. They opt to change textbooks, double time spent on specific subjects, reduce teachers to reading "error-proof" (read "teacher-proof") scripts, multiply standards, add test practice days, hold bribe days for higher test scores, play games with multiple intelligences, and look for any number of other quickly affixed band-aides.

Two reasons explain why professional development is so often bypassed in favor of more serious and substantive solutions for the continuous low-performance problem. Both reasons are covered by a superficial game of blame. The game starts when those who already have a shallow regard for teachers reject professional development solutions because they believe at least one of the following:

a. Teachers don't have sufficient brainpower to work with these challenging learners.

b. Teachers lack the motivation to solve the problem.

c. Teachers hate change.

d. Teachers prefer quick fixes.

The blame game, too often voiced by politicians, community leaders, and others who fall for the "if you can't do, you teach" myth, further ignores that times change, student populations change, knowledge of best practices change, and knowledge of how to best meet the needs of student populations for which many teachers were never prepared change. It is faster and cheaper, they believe, to go with the latest fad for fixing the issue as soon as possible, than it is to think through the process in search of substantive solutions that only more effective teachers can provide.

Most pointedly, the blame game fails to recognize that teachers are faced with increasing numbers of students who do not believe they themselves can learn. Without having the quality resources and time that will provide teachers with the ability to respond to these challenges, it is likely that most teachers, as too many novice teachers already do, will sink in the swamp of frustration. The dramatic and deep changes that have impacted education require that teachers—like adult learners in medicine, law, business, and science—be given the type of learning experiences that have the highest chance of payoff via vastly improved instruction. Such experiences provide the motivation teachers need to do the hard work of changing students hearts, minds, and behaviors.

The Teacher-Proof Insult

The second argument that paints teachers as unmotivated, uninterested, and thus incapable of meeting the needs of the more difficult students to teach is also not new. The "teacher proof" curriculum concept has deep roots. More recently, teacher-proof instruction has become a password most uttered by textbook publishers for improving instruction, especially for those student groups identified in federal legislation as "left behind."

A COMPARISON TO OTHER PROFESSIONS

Other professions take a different tack when faced with new and difficult problems such as those faced by teachers in today's classrooms. Take the science research community as one example. It is a community that faces prodigious challenges: global warming, starvation of vast populations, weapons of mass destruction, disease pandemics, and so on. As early as their undergraduate years, science students are introduced to the process of investigation—the search for answers to the problems being studied by their major professors. In graduate studies, they continue this search. They are not presented with the correct answers or saturated with the latest theories. They are not given scripted solutions. By the time they proceed to full work in their profession, be it located in a lab, an office or a field study, young scientists have become lifelong askers of the deepest questions.

"It's almost perfect. We just need to tweak the script."

TARGETING LEARNING NEEDS OF THE STRUGGLING STUDENTS

What are the learning needs of the most struggling students? Assessors can look at the needs of these students as they would look at the layers of an iceberg (see Figure 3.1). These layers become evident as a glacier melts and "calves." The exposed sides of the iceberg show the years of accumulated snow as layers in a cake. It is the top layer that first strikes the eye. As teachers dig deeper, the student needs become more and more difficult to find, but also more and more important to pinpoint. Like fish feeding in an iceberg, the greatest challenge for teachers is to find what is below the surface.

Assessing Basic Skill Deficiencies

Social, economic, and political pressures have put a spotlight on the basic skill deficiencies of struggling learners. Without the basic skills needed to understand the printed

Figure 3.1   Layers of the Iceberg

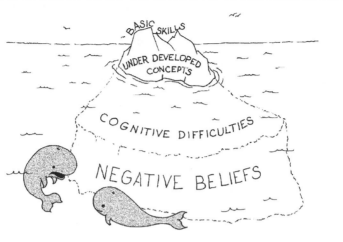

"The iceberg goes deeper than I thought."

word, to express themselves, or to do basic math calculations, students will struggle in other academic areas as well.

While basic skill assessments are completed at the end of each school year, delays in receiving the test results may prevent teachers from making use of the information. From the earliest grades, however, teachers can create easy-to-repeat assessments at each quarter of the school year by using district standards and benchmarks joined with their own experiences. For example, in reading, they can first select the standard such as "Students will read and understand grade appropriate material. They will draw upon a wide variety of comprehension strategies as needed (e.g., generating and responding to essential questions, making predictions, comparing information from several sources)" (California Content Standards, Language Arts, Grade 4). Next, the teachers ask questions such as "What do we see and hear that tells us this student is not performing as expected?" "Is she a strategic thinker?" "Does she use a variety of strategies?" "If not, what creates the most difficulty?" Similar questions for writing and mathematics with the responses placed on a plus-minus T-chart (see Figure 3.2) will gather data that is indicative of the immediate and critical basic skill needs. Such information provides solid data at the time when teachers can study and use it. There is no need for the teachers to wait forever for delivery of the standardized test results.

Figure 3.2   T-Chart

Standard: (seventh grade, sample, mathematics) Students express quantitative relationships by using algebraic terminology, expressions, equations, inequalities, and graphs.

Plus	Minus
1. Uses variables	1. Uses algebraic terms
2. Uses appropriate operation	2. Uses graphs to represent quantities
3. Uses algebraic expressions	3. Interprets graphs

In the upper grades, a key teacher-made launch question for basic skill analysis on a quarterly T-chart will help the teachers pinpoint the deficiencies they need to address. When focusing on the basic skills, all faculty who work with these students should engage in this search for the most telltale basic skill deficiencies. For instance, in a middle school, each house team can pose the same question for students. "What are we seeing/not seeing and hearing/not hearing that tells us students need help with writing strategies?" At a high school, cross disciplinary teams can be formed from departments that make high use of a specific set of standards-based basic skills. These teams can then gather the data with a jigsaw assessment (e.g., math, science, art, and practical arts collaborate on math needs identification). The size of each piece of the puzzle will approximate the seriousness of the need (see Figure 3.3).

Peer teams divide the topics and gather data from all teachers in the department. After combining the data from each team (thus the name "jigsaw"), the team analyzes the data as they look for evidence of the most common difficulties. They

Figure 3.3   Upper Grade Assessment Jigsaw

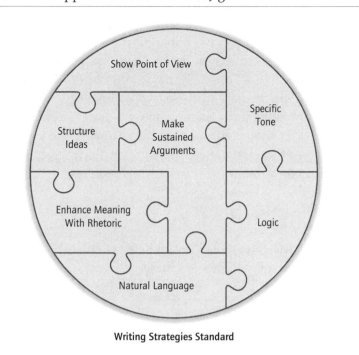

Writing Strategies Standard

end by creating a priority list for those deficiencies that require the most immediate or most sustained attention (see Figure 3.4).

Figure 3.4   Priority Ladder

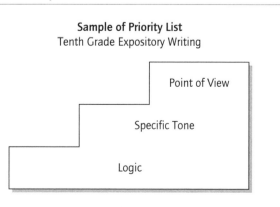

Sample of Priority List
Tenth Grade Expository Writing

Assessing Undeveloped and Misunderstood Concepts

The subject-based assessment of students' understanding of important curricular concepts will expose a different collection of deficiencies: the essential concepts students are expected to learn (e.g., "fractions" in math, "mobius" in chemistry, "migration" in social studies). Most usually, the concept assessment begins with teachers from a department or subject area studying their content standards and using a rubric to assess their students' conceptual understandings of the most important concepts in the curriculum (see Figure 3.5).

Figure 3.5   Twelfth Grade Content Standard: American History and Economics—A Sample Rubric

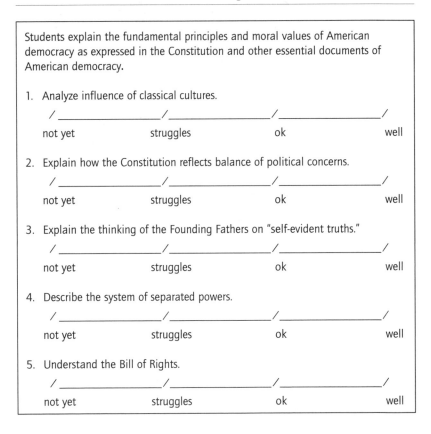

Students explain the fundamental principles and moral values of American democracy as expressed in the Constitution and other essential documents of American democracy.

1. Analyze influence of classical cultures.

    /_____/_____/_____/
    not yet   struggles   ok   well

2. Explain how the Constitution reflects balance of political concerns.

    /_____/_____/_____/
    not yet   struggles   ok   well

3. Explain the thinking of the Founding Fathers on "self-evident truths."

    /_____/_____/_____/
    not yet   struggles   ok   well

4. Describe the system of separated powers.

    /_____/_____/_____/
    not yet   struggles   ok   well

5. Understand the Bill of Rights.

    /_____/_____/_____/
    not yet   struggles   ok   well

The most easily accessed student data to answer these concept questions is found in the students' daily work. After a knowledge test that includes questions about a core concept such as "mitosis" in biology or "democracy" in U.S. history, teachers can use the test data to analyze the most common misconceptions and ascertain which questions are most troublesome for the lowest quartile of students.

Assessing Cognitive Deficiencies

"I tried that; it doesn't work" is an often-heard refrain from teachers who work with struggling students. The "thats" are multiple. "Thats" can include tips from a colleague responding to "What do I do with this student who . . . ?" in an informal lounge discussion; ten tactics outlined in a workshop for "Motivating the Slow Learner;" or a new tip to use a "best practice" such as cooperative learning, graphic organizers, or summaries.

"Thats" can come from the best of teachers using the best of instruction. Regardless, there are times, with a single student or a whole class, when nothing seems to work for this teacher. The students' performance in mastering basic skills or developing key concepts stays static, frozen on a plateau that never seems to move.

The Plateau Effect

The "plateau effect" is most noticeable when what "works" in helping many students understand a concept, master a skill, complete a task, or solve a problem does not initiate *performance* change in some students. From a whole class perspective, the plateau stands out when teachers have gathered data carefully, analyzed it, and noticed that in spite of their best efforts, certain students' tests bottom out week-in and week-out. No changes in knowledge. No changes in skill.

When the data shows students on this learning plateau, all is not lost. The plateau is a signal for the teachers to dig deeper in their needs assessment and take a look at the third level of student need: cognitive deficiencies.

Identifying Cognitive Deficiencies

What is a cognitive deficiency? First theorized by Jean Piaget (1972) and then developed by Reuven Feuerstein (2006), a cognitive deficiency is an undeveloped or missing cognitive function that inhibits learners from developing the thinking operations called executive functions. When a cognitive operation such as hypothesizing, comparing, or summarizing is blocked by one or more deficiencies, then the students' learning is blocked and the students remain in a condition of inefficient learning.

Feuerstein is careful to point out the distinction between those who teach that cognitive deficiencies are fixed and unchangeable versus those who teach that teachers can change these conditions. He bases his teaching about cognitive deficiencies, their possible causes, and their plasticity on evidence gathered in more than 2000 studies, including a growing number of brain studies. He writes that in spite of etiology

"I thought you said we'd be off the plateau by now."

(genetic shortcomings as with Down Syndrome and Fragile X children), cultural deprivation (children who are deprived of access to their cultural heritage), economic deprivation (young children who are deprived of mediated learning experiences from their impoverished parents) and special needs (learning disabilities, behavioral disabilities, etc.), with the right type of mediated learning experience, teachers and other caregivers can develop these students' cognitive capabilities and strengthen these students' ability to think, to problem solve, and to learn. In this context, Feuerstein teaches that it must be clear that the word "deficiency" describes only a condition that teachers can change. Such conditions, he emphasizes, are not permanent.

When traditional efforts to correct basic skill deficiencies and shallow conceptual understandings fall flat, as happened with Tim (see Figure 3.6), teachers can turn to a cognitive

Figure 3.6   Timothy's Story

> When Tim arrived at Kingston Middle School, he was already three years behind in reading and math. He did not hide his dislike for school, but he loved hanging out with his friends. When he went home, he never brought his homework. When asked, he answered, "I don't have none" as he ran off to play his video games.
>
> This year, one thing was different. He was living in a new foster home, and his new dad didn't believe Tim's story. After the first teacher conference night, Tim knew he was in trouble.
>
> Tim's dad was furious when he came home from the conference. Tim decided that the best thing to do was not make him madder. He could get kicked out of another home and he didn't want that. So, he agreed to everything his foster dad said. He would do homework every night. He would not shout out in class and he would keep his locker and desk in order. No more wrinkled and crumbled papers. No more guessing just to get the page done. He would think before he acted.
>
> Three years later, it was time for Tim to graduate. He was so nervous—he was giving the valedictorian speech, and, as eighth grade class president, he had to present the class present to the principal. He decided to talk about his journey from being a loser to being a champ.
>
> Tim remembered how it was in math class. After he showed he really didn't know any math, Mr. Moore had given him three goals. Every day he had to write in his journal how he was more precise, more organized, and getting better at connecting ideas. Tim explained how Mr. Moore had said his problems in math weren't that he didn't understand. "It was my sloppy thinking and disorganization," Tim shared with his audience. Mr. Moore also had told Tim that when he got better at thinking in an organized way and being precise, the math would follow. "It turned out he was right. And his ideas helped me in my other classes too."

assessment. With the understanding that the means do exist for helping these students get off the plateau, teachers can use the cognitive assessment to target the functions that need development.

Mr. Moore saw Tim's plateau. He also saw Tim's deficient functions: rampant impulsivity, imprecision and inaccuracy, disorganization, and episodic thinking. He employed the simple method of turning Tim into a goal planner who was reflective, precise, and organized by having Tim attend to his own thinking and then use that thinking to build habits of mind that he could apply to his daily school work.

Teachers can start their assessment of those students for whom even the best traditional skills and concepts efforts have fallen short by changing the quality of the students' learning experiences. When teachers want to change the quality of students' thinking, they highlight the development of the cognitive functions (see Figure 3.7). As students focus on

Figure 3.7   A Starter List of Cognitive Deficiencies and Efficiencies

Cognitive Deficiency	Cognitive Efficiency
Episodic	Makes Cognitive Connections
Impulsive	Stops and Thinks Before Acting
Disorganized	Organized Work Habits
Illogical	Selects Relevant Information
Self-Centered	Sees Other Points of View
Unsystematic	Sets Goals and Plans
Imprecise	Attends to Details
Inaccurate	Records and Reports All Facts
Literal	Interprets and Infers

the functions they need to develop, the new focus gradually eats away at their negative thinking behaviors and helps the students develop the habits of thinking needed to rise off the plateau of negative belief.

For each of these cognitive deficiencies, teachers can brainstorm together with a T-chart on the most observable cognitive misbehaviors. What do these students do? What do they say? What do we want them to say and do? Consider the samples in Figure 3.8 and Figure 3.9.

Figure 3.8   Sample T-Chart: Impulsivity

Does	Says
Skips instructions	Shouts out answers
Doesn't read question	Interrupts others
Jumps from idea to idea	
Doesn't think about consequences	

Figure 3.9   Sample T-Chart: Disorganized Thinking

Does	Says
Skips parts of task and repeats solution	Wild or random guesses
Hit and miss exploration	Hit and miss answers
Can't decide where to start	
Confused about sequence and order	
Episodic planning	

After identifying the behaviors for each cognitive deficiency, the teachers can make charts that allow them to rate (as in a rubric) the frequency of the observation for one or more students (see Figure 3.10). An analysis of these charts will provide a guiding beacon for developing strategies and tactics to move the students across the scale from highly deficient to highly efficient.

Figure 3.10   Sample Rating Chart: Precision

/--	/---/
Jumps around	Looks for exact answer
/--	/---/
Never checks	Double checks answers
/--	/---/
Digresses	Avoids digression
/--	/---/
Mixes details	Attends to details
/--	/---/
Locates inexact details	Locates exact labels

Assessing Negative Belief Systems

The most difficult, but most essential, assessment for changing students' learning dispositions is the assessment of low performing students' beliefs that they cannot learn. These students, the most long-term and stubborn low performers, have formed an understanding with themselves that they cannot succeed in school. They may manifest these negative beliefs with a variety of negative behaviors. Some go silent and sullen. They burrow themselves in anonymity in the back of the classroom. Others act out. They challenge the teacher. They deride attempts of peers who learn more easily. They make fun of the motivated students. Still others clown around making light of the learning they are not doing, and taking outspoken pride in their most obvious cognitive deficiencies. Finally, there are those that just quit, drop out, or allow themselves to be pushed out after an accumulation of various infractions.

Peers, parents, and siblings can reinforce the students' negative learning beliefs. Too often, students hear negative reinforcers such as, "You are as dumb as your brother was," "Keep it up and you'll likely fail as a garbage collector," or "Your best bet is pickpockets' school."

Reversing students' negative beliefs, then, is a monumental task. The task begins by an assessment of low performing students' attitudes about what they can or cannot do in the classroom. A simple rating scale is a place to start. The scale can include inquiry about students' feelings toward school as well as their attitudes toward basic skills, concepts, subject areas, and cognitive deficiencies. Such a scale works best when at least one teacher who has contact with a consistently low performing student reviews the scale with the student and probes for the student's thinking and feeling about the most salient items.

More often than not, prior needs data collected on basic skills or concept assessments, misbehavior, test scores, and grades will have told the teachers all they need to know about a student's negative beliefs toward school. It is likely that the student has already "volunteered" the needed information in word or deed.

In a school filled with low and reluctant performers, teachers can coordinate belief assessments with the data from prior basic skills or cognitive assessments. After amassing this data, they are better prepared to form a plan that will address the need to change belief systems directly.

What might follow-up assessment questions sound like? The most effective are those that challenge the students to think more deeply about the reasons behind their thoughts and feelings toward success and failure in school, goals, and prompts to adjust their course in life. By recording the responses or having students journal responses, the teacher obtains important data for assessing the depth of the beliefs.

SUMMARY POINTS

1. It is important to develop a comprehensive portrait of low performing students' learning needs so that teachers have a complete picture.

2. Students can plateau in their learning in spite of the teachers' use of the best approaches to instruction.

3. When students plateau, it is important for the assessment to consider other deeper levels of need including an assessment of cognitive deficiencies and negative beliefs.

4. Many students' beliefs are so negative toward learning that teachers must help students change these beliefs before they can change their knowledge and skills.

Transfer

A Different Way of Learning

Learners are motivated when they see the usefulness of what they are learning and when they can use that information to do something that has an impact on others.

—D. L. McCombs (1996)

Beth looked at her students' test scores. She was not happy.

The first section of the test asked students to recall information about cognition. The results were impressive. Not a score below 82. The next two sections were not so great. These were her top-grade students. The scores showing understanding of the concepts dropped into the sixties. The transfer section was worse. The best score was a 54.

"What's wrong?" she asked herself. "I gave them the information. They did their research. Why don't they understand?"

THE CHALLENGE OF LEARNING TRANSFER
IN PROFESSIONAL DEVELOPMENT

When professional development programs are built on the understanding that the goal is the transfer of learning into classroom practice, school districts get a far higher return on their investment. Learning transfer, however, doesn't come from happenstance. It requires an intentional plan that starts with the design of learning opportunities that best enable teachers to put into daily practice the concepts they develop during the learning process. It also requires that professional developers create conditions in the workplace that facilitate learning transfer.

THE BEHAVIORIST VIEW

Behaviorists do not accept the concept of learning transfer. Their point of view paints professional development as if it were a schoolhouse with many separate grades and classrooms. In each classroom, a lone teacher faces her children. There are no possible connections to past learning. All that the students learn, they learn as isolated chunks of information. Math is not science. Literature is not music. Art is not math.

In the behaviorist model, teachers attend an institute day program that provides a myriad of different, rarely connected workshops. During the day, teachers are invited to taste from a smorgasbord. Workshops with such topics as "Stress Management" or "Your Retirement Services" address teachers' personal needs; others, such as "Differentiated Instruction With Make and Take Art Projects" or "Brain-Based Learning for Autistic Children," address their professional "wants" for hot topics.

A NEW VIEW

In response to minimal learning transfer, Robin Fogarty (1989) pointed out the weakness of the behaviorist model for educators. In a research project with thirty secondary teachers, she investigated to what degree single workshops lead to classroom application of new ideas. After forty hours of instruction in which the teachers were exposed to new practices for teaching critical thinking, she followed the teachers' implementations in their classrooms. During the workshop, the teachers were asked to become facilitators who established conditions that would promote student thinking and mediators who guided students in the use of more skillful thinking in their coursework. The teachers were encouraged to abandon their current practice of dispensing information.

Fogarty taught by modeling the instructional strategies that she wanted the teachers to use. After the teachers had participated in the model lesson, she guided them through a reflective analysis that ended with specific classroom plans for each strategy. The strategies included cooperative learning, graphic organizers, metacognitive prompts, and "higher-order" questions.

After the workshop, Fogarty observed the teachers in their classrooms. Based on her observation results, she created six categories that described the varying levels of transfer that occurred (see Figure 4.1). The transfer categories ranged from those Fogarty described as "ostriches" who missed opportunities to make transfer to the "soaring" eagles who made substantive changes in their teaching.

From this study, Fogarty identified the different ways that teachers transferred what they learned in a traditional workshop that included modeling, analysis, reflection, and guided planning. She also demonstrated that transfer does happen when the right conditions are created.

CONSTRUCTIVISTS AND TRANSFER

Constructivists view learning transfer as the most complex and important element in the adult learning process (see Figure 4.2 on page 39). Without transfer either by hugging (an immediate connection within a topic or course) or bridging

Figure 4.1   Teacher Levels of Transfer

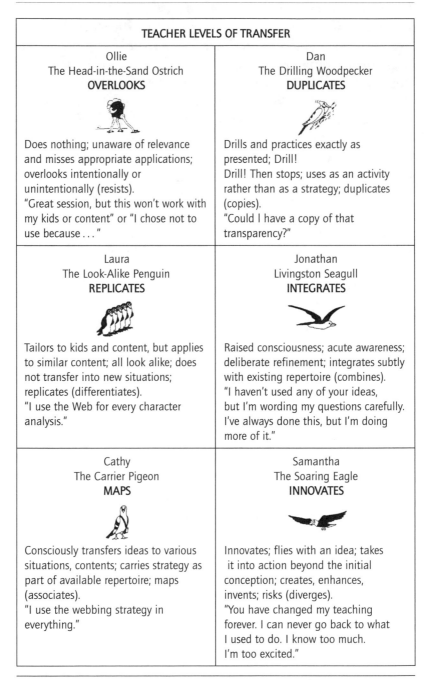

TEACHER LEVELS OF TRANSFER	
Ollie The Head-in-the-Sand Ostrich **OVERLOOKS**	Dan The Drilling Woodpecker **DUPLICATES**
Does nothing; unaware of relevance and misses appropriate applications; overlooks intentionally or unintentionally (resists). "Great session, but this won't work with my kids or content" or "I chose not to use because . . . "	Drills and practices exactly as presented; Drill! Drill! Then stops; uses as an activity rather than as a strategy; duplicates (copies). "Could I have a copy of that transparency?"
Laura The Look-Alike Penguin **REPLICATES**	Jonathan Livingston Seagull **INTEGRATES**
Tailors to kids and content, but applies to similar content; all look alike; does not transfer into new situations; replicates (differentiates). "I use the Web for every character analysis."	Raised consciousness; acute awareness; deliberate refinement; integrates subtly with existing repertoire (combines). "I haven't used any of your ideas, but I'm wording my questions carefully. I've always done this, but I'm doing more of it."
Cathy The Carrier Pigeon **MAPS**	Samantha The Soaring Eagle **INNOVATES**
Consciously transfers ideas to various situations, contents; carries strategy as part of available repertoire; maps (associates). "I use the webbing strategy in everything."	Innovates; flies with an idea; takes it into action beyond the initial conception; creates, enhances, invents; risks (diverges). "You have changed my teaching forever. I can never go back to what I used to do. I know too much. I'm too excited."

SOURCE: James Bellanca and Robin Fogarty, *Blueprints for Achievement in the Thinking Classroom*, Third Edition (Thousand Oaks, CA: Corwin Press, 2003), p. 251.

(a wider connection across the curriculum or into life situations), learning is incomplete—all that the learners have is new information stored unused in the attic parts of their brains.

Because transfer moves from the mere gathering of new information to the application of new ideas constructed from the original information, learning transfer cannot be an instructional afterthought or something that happens by accident. It must be a consciously or intentionally planned result of taking *something* (new skill, concept, belief, value) and moving it *somewhere* (across a lesson, unit, course, job) by means of a carefully selected and transfer-producing *somehow* (expectations, problem-based learning, analogies, metacognitive reflections.)

Figure 4.2   Teach for Transfer

Somethings	Somehows	Somewheres
Knowledge	**Hugging—Low Road**	With Content
Skills	Setting Expectations / Modeling	
Concepts	Matching / Problem-Based Learning	
Attitudes	Simulating	Across Disciplines
	Near Transfer	
Principles	**Bridging—High Road**	
Dispositions	Anticipating Applications / Parallel Problem Solving	Into Life
Criteria	Generalized Concepts / Metacognitive Reflection	
	Using Analogies	
	Far Transfer	

SOURCE: From Robin Fogarty, David Perkins, & John Barell (1992). *The Mindful School: How to Teach for Transfer.* Palatine, IL: IRI/Skylight Publishing, p. 99.

Transfer Is a Two-Way Street

Michael Fullan's (2007) studies on the new meaning of educational change make it apparent that organizational factors can play a major role in promoting learning transfer as a systemic, organizational change process. Just as Fullan notes, *there is no organizational change without individual change*, Bellanca notes that *there is no individual change without organizational change* (as cited in Costa, Bellanca, & Fogarty, 1992). Bellanca's studies on learning transfer's important role in professional development, especially in low performing schools, reinforce the importance of the two-way street connection between organizational and individual change.

Learning Transfer in Systemic Reform

In the systemic construct, the concepts of organizational change and individual change are woven like a fine rug; pull one thread and the entire rug unravels. Just as the multicolored threads in a rug are part of a system, so too are the elements of change in an organization. As individuals construct new ways to teach as a result of a professional learning experience, the system must develop new opportunities to support the transfer of learning. For instance, if teachers learn the importance of such best practices as cooperative learning, nonlinguistic representations, and comparing in the traditional staff development or inservice construct, they have the choice, when they return to the classroom, to use or not use these methods.

In the learning transfer construct, professional developers prepare follow-up activities such as peer coaching, action research projects, or problem-based learning teams that support the teachers' trial applications of these methods. To assist, the principal schedules time for the teams to meet and encourages the teachers to adjust their teaching schedules by selectively abandoning (Costa, 1991) classroom practices that are not as effective as the promising innovations.

While promising, success with learning transfer is a two-edged sword. On the one hand, successful transfer is intentionally enacted by a learner who has gathered new information, integrated that new information with prior knowledge, and planned the best use of the information in the classroom. On the other hand, the professional development specialist, the organization's facilitator of the transfer process, makes changes in the school's culture so that the school is ready to promote the results of the learning transfer. If the culture is hostile or indifferent to the expectation and goals of learning transfer, even the most determined teachers will become frustrated.

THE PROFESSIONAL DEVELOPER AS MEDIATOR OF TRANSFER

Reuven Feuerstein's (2006) Theory of Mediated Learning Experiences shows how teachers who are changing how they instruct add an important dimension to the concept of learning transfer. Feuerstein teaches the importance of learning mediators who assist in the transfer process. The mediator does not wait for the learner to arrive at a specific stage of development. Instead, the mediator speeds the learning process by intervening and creating a need in the learner to learn in four ways. The mediators always:

1. Make clear their intentions to engage the learner.

2. Win a reciprocal engagement from the learner.

3. Emphasize the meaning of the learning experience.

4. Help the adult learner understand the transcendent principles imbedded in the learning.

Summarizing is a high-effect instructional strategy that has a strong impact on student achievement (Marzano et al., 2001). In her lesson with the teachers, Ms. Burke (Figure 4.3) began by making clear her *intention* to help the teachers understand the concept. She used two tactics: she stated her intention and she wrote it on the newsprint.

Asking questions, Ms. Burke engaged the teachers in a dialogue about the key concept. To promote the teachers' reciprocity

Figure 4.3   Ms. Burke's Story

> *"Today,"* Ms. Burke began, as she wrote the word *"summary"* on the newsprint, *"my intent is that we understand the components or attributes of a summary... Who can help me by explaining what they know about the concept, summary?"*
>
> Ms. Burke waited. Several teachers raised their hands. She continued to wait. More hands went up.
>
> *"Merri?"* Ms. Burke asked.
>
> *"I think it comes from the idea of 'sums'. So it means 'added up ideas.' We write down all the ideas on a topic,"* Merri explained.
>
> *"That is a great start. Who can add to it?"* Ms. Burke asked. *"Hilary?"*
>
> *"A good summary is like a good paragraph,"* Hilary added. *"It has a thesis and supporting ideas."*
>
> *"Very good,"* responded Ms. Burke, her voice filled with sparkle. *"Now who can make a summary of these points? We have all the material, I think, to understand what we mean by this word. Join with a partner where you are and agree on a definition. Then we will share ideas and refine it."*

she added the tactics of wait time, distribution of responses, and positive feedback. When she observed sufficient clarity in responses, Ms. Burke used pairs to build sample summaries that would define or give meaning to the word. Then, the only criterion left for mediating a learning experience was *transcendence*. She would next urge her students to frame the definition of summary so that they could generalize the definition and apply it to many different types of summaries.

By adding the criteria as the measuring sticks of a learning experience that ends with full transfer, professional developers prepare their gardens for growing a new bed of roses. Intentionality and reciprocity, meaning, and transcendence are the vital nutrients needed to produce large and colorful blossoms.

Transfer: A Key to Change

Learning transfer is the key to both individual change and organizational change. When adult learners, especially teachers, are challenged to abandon reliance on a passive mode of instruction and pushed to become active generators with their knowledge (Feuerstein, 2006), they discover the joy and the responsibility of intrinsic motivation. Learning experiences grounded by the criteria initiate this shift as the learners become active seekers of information. Instead of sitting and listening to experts in a lecture hall, the active learners switch information gathering to active research, question posing, and investigation. Instead of waiting to take notes on new ideas and then regurgitate or reject them, the learners take responsibility for their own mental engagement in the construction of new knowledge. Becoming increasingly aware that active learning not only requires information gathering, but also understanding and application of this information, teacher-learners assume a greater professional responsibility for making sure that every student benefits. Instead of participating in one- to five-day workshops designed to "fix" them, teachers empower themselves to transform new understandings into strong action plans that enrich the learning of their students.

This process does not come without challenges. As teachers empower themselves to use the new knowledge, they can run into systemic obstacles, which block their transmission of their new insights and plans to students. The first of these is the daily classroom regimen. If teachers are going to add cooperative learning to their instructional repertoires, their first attempts will eat up time that is not available in the already-packed day. If they are going to revise reading instruction to make use of comparing and hypothesizing—two of the high-impact strategies that most influence achievement—they will have to curtail other less effective strategies such as sustained silent reading or choral reading.

In many schools, teachers do not have a choice of strategies they can use. Some principals hand out scripts that dictate the words and time allotments for reading or math instruction. Will they have permission to deviate from the norm? Or will they be told, stick to the script? In some districts, even the principal cannot grant that permission.

THE PROFESSIONAL DEVELOPER AS
CHAMPION OF CHANGE

In the application stage, it is the professional developer who has the most opportunity to champion the changes. Among the champion roles, one of the most important is that of challenger and collaborator. In this role, the professional developer must lead the charge to change the system so that the system is adaptable to the practice of transfer. Professional developers must be ready to stand up against those systemic practices that prevent teachers from moving through the transfer process as they innovate, refine, and agree to sustain new best practices. These developers must also be ready to collaborate with principals and central office administrators to move any rocks of opposition and resistance out of the pathway.

When the professional developers adopt these roles to become champions for change they must shine both sides of the change coin. They will enable teachers and administrators to collaborate in using the best practices that enrich their students' learning experiences and they will work to institutionalize professional development best practices for supporting the teacher change.

BEST PRACTICES THAT
PROMOTE LEARNING TRANSFER

Regardless of the size of a school or the financial status of the district, professional developers can champion systemic change. The concept of learning transfer is the most important ingredient in making the changes that result in higher student achievement throughout a school or district. To promote learning transfer, there are a variety of strategies, some of which may already be used in the school. Over the past twenty years, in fact, the number of these best practices of professional development might be nominated for a "Hall of Fame."

Peer Coaching

In 1983, Beverly Showers and Bruce Joyce laid the foundation for learning transfer as the principle outcome of any of the models of teaching. In addition to identifying the need for effective peer coaching for *all* professional development efforts, their landmark study provided a research-rich defense for the validity of learning transfer in all adult learning opportunities. By implication, they condemned as financially wasteful those inservice practices that did little more than entertain or provide information and waste teachers' time.

This study detailed the effects/noneffects of inservice activities that were limited to presentations of concepts and theories, demonstrations of practices, and the microteaching in a workshop (see Figure 4.4). As a result of such commonly

Figure 4.4   Effects of Staff Development

Classroom Application

Training Strategy		Knowledge	Demonstration of Behavior	Transfer to Work Setting
	Presentation of Concepts and Theory	65%	15%	10%
	Demonstration of Behavior	85%	8%	10%
	Low-Risk Practice With Feedback (Teaching)	85%	80%	15%
	Coaching in Workplace (Behavior and Decisions)	90%	90%	80%

SOURCE: Adapted from Bruce Joyce and Beverly Showers (1988). *Student Achievement Through Staff Development*. New York: Longman, p. 71.

used approaches, the researchers found that less than 15 percent of those who were taught or trained in this way actually used any part of what was learned. Until peer coaching was added to the mix, the transfer was minimal. Not only did the application rate soar to 80 percent with the addition of peer coaching, but the recall of knowledge and ability to demonstrate the new teaching behavior soared to 90 percent.

In dollars and cents, these figures translate to a $1.00 return on the $10 investment in a workshop and to a $9.00 return on the $10 investment in the learning transfer program. For students, one out of ten classes benefited from the workshop; nine out of ten benefitted from the transfer program.

Cognitive Coaching

Arthur Costa and Robert Garmston (1985) expanded Joyce and Showers' coaching study. In their work on cognitive coaching, these adult educators promoted the practice of mediation in professional learning experiences for educators. They prepared coaches to keep the teachers' thinking at the "center of the change universe." As the coaches probe teachers' thinking about their classroom practice, they ask thought-provoking questions about theory and practice. Additional questions lead the teachers to think about the transfer of their thinking into classroom practices. As is appropriate for all mediated learning experiences, the coaches' questions asked teachers to clarify their intent in using a practice, to explain the meaning and the justification for the practice, and to explain how they would make the practice transcend simple tasks. Coaches also asked questions to develop teachers' feelings of competence, self-regulation, and determination.

Metacognitive Mediation

Metacognition or "thinking about thinking" is a reflective process that was advanced by Reuven Feuerstein in the late

60s. In his Theory of Structural Cognitive Modifiability (2006), Feuerstein posited how learners, guided by the skilled mediator's questions that filter distractions from the thinking process, could take greater control of what or how they were thinking.

In the mid-80s, Palincsar and Brown (1986) applied the practices and principles of Feuerstein's metacognitive theory to the practice of reading. They researched a model of cognitive interaction that enabled one learner to ask questions of another. The questions developed the skills of clarification, paraphrasing, predicting, and summarizing.

In 1991, Fogarty applied the principles to a wide range of instructional tactics. In her models of integrated learning, she promoted metacognition as the key tool by which students could connect ideas together. When training teachers, Fogarty relied on a variety of metacognitive tools including De Bono's (1992) PMI chart (see Figure 4.5) and Bellanca's (as cited in Fogarty, 1991) "Questions from Mrs. Potter."

With metacognition, the adult learners reflect on their thinking processes before, during, and after a task that they wish to transfer. These reflections, sometimes recorded in a journal, are the primary tool that the learner uses to assess and reflect on the performance of a task.

Figure 4.5   De Bono's PMI Chart

Launch Question: How might you evaluate the quality of your use of the hypothesizing strategy in this week's science lessons?

Pluses	Minuses	Interesting Questions

Shepherding

Feuerstein's practices for mediated learning experiences and coaching are premier ingredients in the concept of *shepherding* described by Salomon and Perkins (1988). In their descriptions of learning transfer, these researchers discuss the passive approach to learning as advocated by Piaget and Montessori. In these approaches, learning is a process in which it is important to "leave the sheep alone" so that they can wander on their own back to the barn. If transfer happens, it is because the learners' natural talents develop unassisted— the learners make transfer on their own. No intervention or guidance from a shepherd is needed.

Salomon and Perkins contrast this natural development or "leave them alone" theory with the theory of Bo Peep who guides the sheep home to the barn. The shepherd mediates the transfer. The shepherd points out the best pathways to the sheep, guides the sheep homeward, and protects them from wolves.

In the context of coaching, the shepherds mediate the learning experience (see Figure 4.6). They don't leave the sheep to find their own way in their own time. The professional developer as shepherd mediates the thinking process by asking critical questions. These questions assist the learners in solving problems and making decisions that produce learning transfer.

Peer Investigations

An investigation is a search for solutions to a problem. The search makes use of data to facilitate the discovery of answers that modify or eliminate the problem. In a peer investigation, teams of two to three teachers identify a problem and gather data that will lead them to possible solutions. They then test the candidate solutions to determine which will be most successful and the best solution. This process is transfer-rich in that the information that the teachers gather on the problem lead them to immediate classroom applications that they must test.

Figure 4.6   Sample Questions to Mediate the Transfer of Learning

Setting Goals for Transfer

1. What are your specific reasons for learning this material? How do you think you might make use of it in your classroom?
2. Among these reasons, what are your priority goals?
3. How will students benefit from these goals?
4. What are the obstacles to your success in reaching these goals?
5. How will you overcome these obstacles that might block your successful transfer?
6. How will you know whether you have achieved these goals?

Monitoring Progress

1. How well are you doing in moving toward each goal?
2. How do you know that?
3. What modifications do you think you might need to make? What have you learned that indicates you might change your goal?
4. How will you change your goal?
5. What details have you thought about that will fit with the new goal?

Assessing the Results

1. How successful were you in achieving your transfer goals?
2. What is your evidence?
3. If you did the same applications in the future, what would you change?
4. How would these changes benefit your students?
5. How would you change your thinking processes in the future?
6. What help do you need from me?

Action Research

Action research is a process of problem solving conducted by teams in a community of best practice. Richard Schmuck (2005) presented several models of successful action research in his pioneering applications of Kurt Lewin's ideas to teacher education. Action research challenges traditional research by engaging teachers in deep reflection about the underlying causes of students' low performance. Using reflective inquiry, the teacher teams seek data to reinforce hypotheses about best practices. Because they are gathering the data from their own performances, learning transfer is high.

Project-Based Learning

In project-based learning (PBL), teachers work in grade-level teams to explore real problems from their classrooms and create presentations that share what they have learned. This approach increases deeper knowledge, motivation, and self-direction as they work on the project within their school.

SUMMARY POINTS

1. Learning transfer results from a purposeful transformation of new information into a unique application.

2. Learning transfer results from changes in the individual and changes in the school organization.

3. Learning transfer is the key that enables teachers to impact student performance with the application of new ideas and programs.

4. There are a variety of transfer-rich approaches that assist professional developers and promote learning transfer from what teachers learn in workshops, or other means of information gathering, to the classroom.

5

Learning Transfer in the Learning Community

Communities of practice . . . operate with a commitment to the norms of continuous improvement and experimentation and engage their members in improving their daily work to advance the achievement of school district and school goals for student learning.

—National Staff Development Council

"We sink or swim together," Roger stated. "We know that this concept applies to student learning in the classroom. The question is 'Does it apply in professional development?'"

"I don't see why not," David answered. "We have always followed that principle in our work together."

(Continued)

(Continued)

"I agree," said Roger. "Positive interdependence is important, maybe more important, when adults learn together."

"Yes, but it is not an easy task. Teachers especially are used to working alone with the doors to their classrooms shut. It takes time and expertise to form a community of learners."

"I agree to that also," added Roger. "And I can think of no better way than to build a community of practice. Teachers study a common practice, design lessons, and then help each other refine the practice. The more often they work together, the more they will bond with positive interdependence. After success with one practice, they can move to another. This gives them the common goal to share and compare what they think makes each practice work."

BUILDING TRANSFER WITHIN A COMMUNITY OF LEARNERS

The transfer-promoting school becomes a learning community when it builds its professional development programs on the expectations that all learning is for transfer. In this context, the professional developer facilitates the transformation of the school's culture with an expectation that all staff transfer what they learn in their professional development programs into their daily work. All decisions are based on whether or not all children, especially those who have struggled the most to learn, will leave the school better prepared for life in the twenty-first century. The community's learning goals, responding to the needs of the students, align individual applications of new teaching practices and programs with this mission.

THE PRIMACY OF THE LEARNING COMMUNITY

To start a learning community, school leaders choose different pathways. Some take the path of declaring formal policies,

"How long do you think they'll stick together?"

practices, and procedures: "This community will be." Others, as in the academy story (see Figure 5.1), start from the ground floor by providing the staff with concrete experiences that model the expectations for transfer as they learn new practices. As teachers interact positively to learn a practice for transfer to the classroom, they build the learning community.

This second and preferred approach is a paradigm shift for many teachers. However, it makes it easier for the teachers to engage new ideas that they can immediately implement. It puts the locus of responsibility on their shoulders to apply what they are learning in the context of the community's shared goal. Rather than leave innovation to a few risk takers, they find ways to encourage the entire teaching staff to participate in the improvement process and to make their own differentiation choices as they apply what they have learned.

Figure 5.1   A Transfer Story

The students were tough. That is why he had agreed to accept the principal position. The school was a blank tablet. That is the second reason he accepted the job. He could design the school to fit the kids' learning needs.

Having been a social worker before completing his EdD, Chris knew that more of "the same old, same old" would not work with either group. The first group consisted of adolescents with a horrendous drug or alcohol abuse history. Sent by their home districts from all parts of the state, they had just finished their "drying out" program in the psychiatric unit. Now they were his to catch up, turn around, and return to their schools. He welcomed the challenge.

The school's second group's members were also adolescents. But these students would not go to a public high school again. They would live as residents of the academy until they were twenty-one. All were labeled "developmentally disabled." Due to other traumas in their lives, they had come to the academy as a school of last resort. These students, the new principal thought, would be double the challenge.

First, Chris knew he would have to prepare the new staff. Mostly young with little more than five years of special education experience, a strong sense of commitment to students, and an appreciation for his learning community ideas, they were eager to start. In the two weeks prior to the first students' arrival, he outlined the students' daily schedules. The major differences between the two groups would be the student-teacher ratio and the pace of instruction. From the beginning, the principal noted that he would expect all faculty members to work together and apply the ideas they would be learning. He was sure that there was no time for entrepreneurship or personal development. The professional development he had in mind would start with what was good for the students and fit the plan. Not until the teachers each got to their own classrooms would there be any differentiation.

He outlined the program. "In the first two weeks, we are going to study a program that has two purposes. First, we are going to turn these students into learners. To a one, they hate school, have failed at school and were on the way to failing at life. We are changing those beliefs. We'll start by making them more efficient learners. We are going to change their thought patterns and help them get rid of their negative thinking about what they can and cannot do. I want them all taking pride in themselves as good students. Second, we are going to give them a fresh outlook on school. None of them have gotten over the hump with traditional methods. We are going to use lots of projects in math, science, social studies—everywhere—to get them to engage their minds so they can do the expected schoolwork. And lastly, in this next two weeks, we are going to learn how to do all that."

After intense hands-on study in those two weeks, the new faculty welcomed the students. During first period every morning, teachers mediated students' thinking and problem solving. The teachers chose different tools and made the applications fit their students. To the teachers' pleasant surprise, their new students quickly dug into the problem solving tasks and discussed the thinking strategies they were learning. In the subject courses, the students made the bridges into their projects. And in the work-study time, set up on the school grounds, they made the connection among the thinking strategies and the work they were doing.

Not that the days or classes all went smoothly. But the implementation plan covered that too. Once a week, the cognitive skills instructor, Shannon, arrived for a day of on-site coaching and conferencing with the teachers. In their teams, the teachers described their concerns. The instructor coach reviewed, demonstrated, and helped refine. In pairs and groups of three, they left their students while another team "covered" during the coaching time.

"What I like about our professional development," commented Tamara, a group leader, "is the chance to really transfer what we learned right to the students. And having the support from our colleagues and Shannon has made a huge difference. I've had enough inservice in my short teaching career to last a lifetime. This is my first experience where it really makes a difference."

"Ditto," added Todd. "I've learned more about teaching in these few weeks than my four years at Stanford. I am using what I learned here and it really works. I had my doubts, but when Shannon helped us make the tactical check lists, it just brought everything together."

"And everyone," said Kate, the school social worker. "We had to think through those lists ourselves and we bonded as a team. It was a tough task, but really helped. When our principal first told us what he expected, I blanched. I didn't think there was any way this stuff would work with these kids. Was I ever wrong!"

"What we are doing surprised me," said Tamara. "I have always had my professional development separated from the school's improvement goals.

When I got my MA it was personal. I did what I wanted. Here, we are starting with what the kids need and we all build our professional development on those needs. It is swim together or sink. No one differentiates what we are doing ahead of time. We each have to differentiate what we have learned for our students."

Whichever pathway principals choose, they do not have to require a formal study of the theory that underscores a learning community program. They can provide and structure professional development experiences, which immerse the teachers in forming such a community. From these experiences, the teachers and administrators build "the real thing." Thus, a community-based professional development program saturated with transfer practices provides a unique opportunity for "learning by doing."

Teams are important structures for building a successful learning community for transfer program at a school site. The school site, John Goodlad (1994) told educators, is the locus of change. Peter Senge (1990) noted that team leadership of a site's change process creates the most synergy among all participants. At the school site, it is important that site leadership, whether vested in a principal alone or a site-leadership team, assumes the responsibility for creating a faculty synergy beneficial to all students. For this to occur, leadership will organize the site into productive teams committed to the full implementation of the ideas for change they develop. Such team involvement communicates that schoolwide commitment is not only an administrative responsibility, but a responsibility shared by all.

In *The Leader-Manager* (1994), William Hitt describes the characteristics of well-functioning teams. When teams are joined in pursuit of a shared communitywide goal, the same characteristics apply.

> *Common agreement on high expectations for the team.* All members have a will to excel. Primary motivators are high standards, quality, and excellence. Mediocrity is not tolerated.

> *A commitment to common goals.* The goals provide the team members a common focus. All members have a clear understanding of the goals, and they accept them. Further, they realize that the goals can be achieved only through a team effort.

> *Assumed responsibility for work that must be done.* Each member has a defined job but, in addition, has a commitment to do anything that needs doing to achieve the goal. All members of the team have internalized the catch phrase: "If something needs doing, then see to it that it gets done."

> *Honest and open communication.* The members openly express their thoughts and feelings, and they feel free to ask questions with the confidence that they will receive honest answers. There are no hidden agendas; everything is aboveboard between teachers and teachers and between administrators and teachers.

> *Common access to information.* Information is viewed as a vital resource to each member, and it is the leader's responsibility to make certain that every member has the

information needed to carry out plans for attaining the team's goals. There are no secrets or clique-favored channels of information.

A climate of trust. Each team member has an instinctive, unquestioning belief in the other team members. Trust is the glue that holds the group together and enlightened leaders know that trust begets trust.

A general feeling that one can influence what happens. Members of such a team feel confident that they will be listened to by their peers and that their ideas will be taken into consideration.

Support for decisions that are made. On key decisions outside the responsibility of the team, the affected parties are given an opportunity to express their thoughts and feelings about the matters at hand.

A win-win approach to conflict management. In a team, affected parties approach the confrontation with the assumption that each can emerge as a winner. They jointly explore alternative ways in which both parties achieve their goals and learn how they might help the others achieve their goals.

A focus on process as well as results. On a continuing basis, the team members address these questions: (1) How well are we functioning as a team? (2) What barriers are preventing us from being a productive team? and (3) What should we do to become a more productive team?

BEYOND TEAMS: BUILDING SYNERGY IN THE LEARNING COMMUNITY

Yes, synergy is necessary for each well-functioning team to achieve transfer goals. However, building synergy into the learning community is even more important, and even more difficult. Schoolwide implementation of common goals is a long-term synergistic task that starts with defining the school's ultimate goal based on the students' learning needs.

Figure 5.2   The Site Leadership as Coordinator of Study Teams

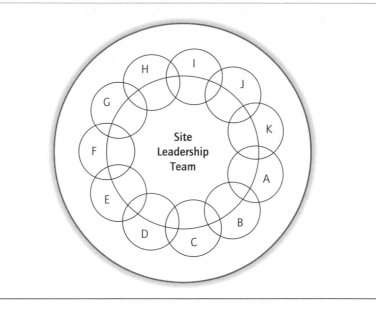

To determine this long-term goal, a site leadership team can construct an annual assessment rubric outlining application standards, short-term goals, and criteria for the school's improvement needs to be created.

The rubric defines expectations for the performances of the individual and the various teams within the community. The rubric also details the strategies and the tools that individuals, teams, and cohort groups should use to gather and weigh assessment data. Individuals' journals, artifacts of student work, lesson designs, and evaluations form the content of portfolios.

In order for synergy to exist, all on the school's site transfer team must carry out their specific responsibilities. The portfolios reflect accomplishments, and the accomplishments give evidence of commitment; but, commitments will vary. The organization shows its commitment by allocating time for information gathering, peer coaching, mentoring, and celebrations. Principals show commitment by encouraging risk taking and providing incentives for attention to application quality. Teachers show commitment by risking attempts at new ways of teaching.

A Focus on Process

Whether developing the teamwork within site teams or creating synergy within a learning community, site leadership teams need to keep everyone's focus on the process of collaboration. The consistent and regular review of the developing synergies gives the best hope for creating the needed bonds among all members. As the site leadership team assesses the process and reviews the products, it is important that the team finds the most practical ways for advancing the spirit that flows through the bonding efforts.

For keeping track of the synergy building or bond process, it is helpful when the site leadership team keeps a record of what is happening. They may develop a community journal that records the historic high points of the transformation, build a database of information that is easily accessed, or select a "historian" to record each year's events based on a rubric created by the site leadership team.

The Professional Developer's Roles

The person assigned the responsibility of leading professional development in a school takes on, or delegates, several roles. In addition to coordinating activities in the school professional development plan, managing the logistics and solving problems that impede the development of the community, the professional development specialist has primary responsibility in three important areas. Attending to these responsibilities should make up the bulk of the developer's time and energy.

Facilitating development of the school teams. In this role, the developer collaborates first with the site leadership team.

The developer coaches the team to develop its process skills for problem solving and leadership. In addition, the developer prepares facilitators for the "practice" teams.

Creating a climate of transfer. Teams of practice are enriched when they can work in a climate that has a single shared improvement goal—the more rigorous and challenging this goal, the more the teams will bond together and produce meaningful results. On a quarterly basis, the developer can guide the improvement of the climate by having the teams think about the transfer goal, assess their strategies and progress, and then determine refinements. By providing teachers with data feedback on the impact of their transferred knowledge at least twice a year, the developer keeps the mission of the learning community in the forefront of each teacher's mind.

Identifying strategies to build a learning community. In this role, the professional developer provides expert advice on helpful practices that promote learning transfer and strengthen the community of learners. Strategies professional developers can include are:

> *Professional development learning center.* A room dedicated to professional development programs should provide an ample supply of training materials (newsprint, markers, a professional development library of print, software, media materials), equipment (overhead, giant screen, VCR, video projector for tape and computer, computer stations), and furniture (group work tables, materials display tables, computer stations, comfortable chairs) for group programs. It should also provide quiet study areas and technology stations for electronic access to information, Internet projects, teleconferencing, and project creation.

> *Posted expectations for transfer.* Posting the school's vision, rubric, criteria for success, and schedules for team meetings allows teachers and administrators to access program information. Visual reminders can be

enhanced with letters from the district office or with videotaped statements by the superintendent or board president encouraging participation in the professional development program. In elementary schools, colorful signs and posters in the faculty lunch area, lounge, or offices give daily reminders of the expectations.

Display of exemplary applications. A bulletin board displaying photos of classroom applications, student artifacts, and end-of-year exhibitions not only communicates the importance of transfer from training, but also provides sample possibilities for those who appreciate visual models.

Visual cues. Charts listing the coaching and mediating skills, problem-solving models, and collaborative guidelines can be displayed. These serve both to remind and to reinforce the expectation of the collaborative problem solving most helpful to the transfer process. Data walls on which each team keeps its data analysis allow for all to review "what is happening."

Review of Expectations for Transfer

At the start of every transfer-based learning experience, it is helpful to have an explicit reminder of the transfer purpose before and throughout the program. The professional development specialist helps the participants switch focus from taking notes and covering the content to reflecting on the experience's content for its application value. By calling attention to the expectation for transfer, the specialist reinforces the value of transfer. Finally, by taking time in the earliest sessions of the experience to have participants set personal goals for transfer, the specialist encourages participants to take responsibility for their own learning and its application to their classrooms.

Individual study projects and team study groups provide a special challenge. In these cases, the participants can work with the principal, a team leader, or a professional development specialist to review the transfer expectation and to design suitable application goals. These expectations are outlined below.

Setting goals for transfer. In teams or alone, each individual beginning a new professional development task will frame goals for transferring the anticipated learning to the job responsibility. The individual goals align with the schoolwide emphasis targeting student performance. These goals only work well if they are attainable, believable, and countable.

Employing tactics that encourage and enable transfer. The team works together to identify tactics that they have used or learned about from the research. These tactics are those specifically that promote transfer. For instance, in a workshop introducing how to mediate cognitive development, the facilitator can lead the group in designing transfer "homework assignments" at the end of each session. At the start of the next session, the facilitator will allow fifteen minutes for peer teams to share the application artifacts resulting from the assignment.

Use of best cognitive practices. Researchers of the transfer of learning in adults often speak in terms of high road and low road methods. Among the high road approaches are many of the classroom strategies that work identified by Marzano and his associates' (2001) study of best practices. Included among these are the cognitive strategies of asking questions, especially those that promote metacognition, comparing, hypothesizing, and using nonlinguistic representations such as graphic organizers. In this day and age of best practice research, it is inconceivable that school teams working to help the most struggling learners and to promote adult learning transfer would not give primary consideration to using these strategies extensively.

Simulation of best practice. When possible, adult learners focused on transfer should engage in a simulation of research-based "best practices." It is important that the instructor or coach model the use of a best practice and engage participants in a simulated experience followed by an analysis of the practice. Then, participants have the opportunity to learn by doing. More importantly, if participants have no prior experience with the practice, the simulation provides them with a reference for designing applications to use with their own students. When individuals and groups are engaged in self-directed study, it is helpful if they can design a practice demonstration for themselves. Observing a colleague using the practice with students or viewing video clips for analysis will help create a helpful mental model.

Guided applications. After the mediated analysis of a best practice, teacher teams, comprised of faculty with similar content specialties or grade-level assignments, modify the observed practice for their students' needs and incorporate it into a lesson or unit. Where there are concerns about changing the curriculum, adult learners can work with familiar materials, including textbooks, as they redesign daily lessons to include the innovations.

Application reflections. In journals, each teacher on a team takes time to reflect about possible applications.

- "A past opportunity for me to use this practice in a lesson was . . ." "A lesson coming up which I could redesign is . . ."
- "A barrier to success for this practice is . . ."
- "A concern I have for using this practice is . . ."
- "A benefit of this practice for my students is. . . .

Selective abandonment. Simulations, guided applications, and reflections require different time schedules than lectures or workbook practice. Team members can help each other integrate new practices into their daily schedules and abandon less important practices. Teachers' concerns about curriculum coverage will decrease, and they can then focus more clearly on helping students understand key concepts and develop new skills.

Encouragement of transfer. When teachers have a familiar, comfortable way of teaching, beginning a new, foreign approach with different methods is a difficult challenge. Facilitators, principals, coaches, and professional developers need to accentuate encouragement. Each time the adult learner expresses concern about using a new idea, it is important to respond, "You can do it!"

Barriers and blocks to transfer. Adult learners, well practiced in their response to a given set of job expectations, are seldom open to a new set of expectations for innovation. As Fullan (2006) points out, they tend to blow out of proportion the perceived and real barriers to implementation. Important tools for aiding the transfer process include discussions with peers who are overcoming barriers, problem-solving sessions specific to real and perceived barriers, and site leadership in removing barriers. De Bono's (1992) PMI graphic organizer is a structured tool that allows teachers to assess barriers and seek alternative paths.

Opportunities to observe and confer. In addition to planning and assessing applications in teams, individuals have the option of inviting peers and/or administrators to observe applications being made in the classroom and to provide positive feedback. Constructive criticism is given only at the invitation of the teacher being observed. The site administrator is responsible for fulfilling requests to schedule these observations.

Self-assessment of transfer goals. Using journals as well as team discussions, professional development specialists can encourage participants to focus a self assessment on the quality of planned applications. When schedules allow staggered sessions, participants can bring artifacts of their applications to the next learning session and share the applications and the assessment of these artifacts with their teams. Positive feedback and support increase team bonding and problem solving. The stronger the bond created in the learning experience, the more successful the continuation of the work teams after the program's formal sessions end.

End-of-year exhibitions. At the end of the school year, each team prepares a public exhibition and/or a demonstration of the applications its members have refined. Other school teams, community members, and parents are invited to attend and join the celebration.

End-of-year conference. Each individual meets with his or her supervisor at a year-end conference. Primary responsibility is placed on the individual to use the portfolio (Burke, Fogarty, & Belgrad, 2007) to demonstrate how he or she reached the personal improvement goals set earlier in the year using the schoolwide rubric.

SUMMARY POINTS

1. Communities of practice or learning communities are an essential strategy to create the climate that best promotes learning transfer.

2. The professional development specialist at a school site plays multiple roles in developing the learning community.

3. There are multiple tactics for the professional developer to use when building a learning community that promotes learning transfer.

The Three Stages of Professional Development for Change

Concepts are not things that can be changed just by someone telling us a fact. We may be presented with facts, but for us to make sense of them they have to fit what is already in the synapses of the brain.

—George Lakoff

MaryAnne was very nervous. It was a big commitment. In her fourth year teaching in the second grade, she felt like she had finally mastered the reading and math programs. The other parts of the day were falling into place, and she was feeling comfortable

66

with her job. Now, with the new science program, she was about to leave this comfort zone and make a big change. It felt just like high school when the coach asked her to switch from basketball to volleyball. She had spent three years getting good at basketball. Volleyball was adding a whole new game. "What would happen with this new science program?" she asked herself. Teaching the kids to do the science experiments was one thing. It was another to teach them how to be problem solvers. This was a whole new world.

In the first years of teaching a new grade or a new subject, teachers put all their energy into learning how to teach the curriculum, how to understand their students, and how to successfully connect all of the parts and pieces that make the school day fit together. They make sense of what they are experiencing by connecting their new knowledge to the little experiences they had when in school or that they gathered in college.

However, before teachers may feel comfortable with their new assignments, another comes roaring down the track like a runaway train. New grade? New students? New text? New curriculum? New tests? Any one of these curveballs can make teachers feel as if they are starting over again. There is no time for comfort. There is not time to absorb and make sense. If they have survived the first year, will they make it through the next?

Sometimes with the changes that washes over teachers, the school district provides professional development that helps the teachers through the rough waters. When a district wants teachers to make best use of a new practice, it may ask its professional developers to intervene. Mentors can provide a listening ear. They mediate the rush of information and guide the young teacher the right way.

However, after the novices become experienced veterans and take greater control of what they are doing, what does a district or school provide as the changes continue to impact the teachers, so that they not only make sense of new knowledge, but select and use those experiences which will most help their children? More importantly, how does the school system ensure that what teachers are learning fits with its need to address issues that are not aligned with what teachers may "want" to learn with what students "need" to learn?

The answer is for teachers and school district administrators to recognize several points:

1. Every school needs a formal professional development program that enables teachers to manage the changes that impact them, and subsequently improve instruction.

2. School leaders help teachers improve instruction by grounding teachers' development in how the teachers can best meet the needs of their students, especially those students who struggle the most to learn.

3. Teacher development helps teachers and students most effectively when it is a planned process that mediates teachers' new learning experiences so that more often than not teachers can transform what they learn into specific actions that will benefit their students' achievement for the long term.

4. The most effective professional development programs that support substantive and lasting change will prepare teachers in three intentionally designed *stages*: (1) pilot innovation, (2) refinement, and (3) sustainment. It is most likely that when these three stages are carefully implemented over a three-five year timeline, the program will impact students in the short run and the long run. When school leaders ignore the need for the three stages, they might as well not plan the professional development. By planning programs that are designed to fail, they do little more than raise teacher stress, increase teacher cynicism ("This too will pass.") and waste valuable and limited professional development

dollars. Instead, research on effective professional development points the way for making sure that the professional development that teachers plan *does* bring change to the quality of teaching and the quality of learning.

The Three Stages

In this age of high accountability, the more traditional professional development practice of teachers selecting what they want to advance their careers (master's degrees, step and scale points) is shifting to an increased focus on students' needs. This focus relies on the understanding that the need for students to increase their academic performance is the driving force of teachers' professional learning experiences. What is deemed best for the individual teacher mastering the art of instruction takes a backseat to what is deemed best for teachers working in an environment where students' needs take precedence.

As professional development becomes more scientific in the ways that it helps teachers make sense of what they are learning and transfer their new learning, it becomes more systematic in applying what research indicates are the most helpful means. One of the most basic changes that characterizes this shift is the intentional promotion of improvements as long-term efforts that not only meet immediate student needs, but allow for continuation of the adopted practices over time. Thus, professional development moves from being a single, isolated inservice day that entertains or meets the immediate wants of teachers to a multiyear search—a planned program for using those best practices that meet the needs of students first in a regular, systematic, and impactful way.

To accomplish the goal of long-term sustainability of best practices, professional development leaders can design their efforts into three stages: the pilot innovation, the refinement of practice, and the establishment of the long-term improvement (see Figure 6.1).

Figure 6.1   Three Stages of Professional Development: The Cycle
of Change

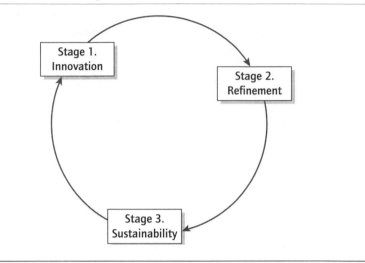

STAGE 1: PILOTING THE INNOVATION

In Stage 1, the professional developer designs a comprehensive learning process that will support the change effort that includes purposeful efforts to accomplish learning transfer. This stage starts from an identified student learning need and ends with teachers seeing the results of their "innovations" in their classrooms. In this stage called "pilot innovation," teachers take the new ideas that they construct about teaching and learning, plan how to integrate these ideas into their classroom teaching, and then gather information on the innovation's degree of success. This stage can last anywhere from six weeks to nine months, depending on its size and scope. For working with an essential instructional tactic such as "wait time," six to eight weeks may suffice; for "trying out" a full strategy such as cooperative learning or hypothetical thinking, an entire school year would be appropriate.

This is a purposeful step-by-step process for learning transfer. Each element in the transfer learning process is connected. There are no isolated episodes—no random acts with one teacher running off to an expensive but unrelated conference and another administrator doing a quick, unconnected study that will gain recertification points but little impact on the school's improvement.

Consider this example of a Stage 1 professional development effort. In an early childhood school, teachers who had determined that their students needed a jumpstart on strengthening key "learning how to learn" skills decided to adopt a program that developed their students' cognitive functions. Because the teachers surmised that their children not only needed to improve their cognitive skills but also needed to make a deep change in their beliefs about their learning capabilities, the teachers selected an intervention that would require thirty minutes per day. To make the program work, the school team planned to move step-by-step through the three phases of learning. These three phases, articulated by Feuerstein (2006) in his essential learning theory, interlock. However, for planning purposes, the team broke the phases into three parts so that they could ensure themselves that they would avoid an impulsive prejudgment of how well the intervention might or might not work with "our students."   Instead, they would wait and see its effects on "our children" as the best way to make an intelligent decision about the intervention's value.

Phase 1: Gathering the Information

After determining which cognitive functions they needed to address for *their* students—in this case impulse control, precision, and orientation in space—the teachers selected their instructional strategies. This collaborative information gathering marked the first *phase* of the innovation *stage* (see Figure 6.2). Also noting that their students' math performance fell into the lowest quartile on the international charts, they worked together to examine what they could do to enrich the students' early thinking in math. They also developed ideas for bridging the learning-to-learn that students would be learning across the curriculum, adding specific applications for developing early concepts in mathematics.

Figure 6.2   Making Sense of the Pilot Innovation

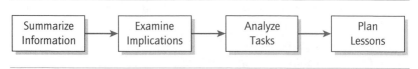

In the first quarter of the year, the teachers scheduled use of the strategies for thirty minutes each day. Each week, the teachers in grade-level teams reviewed the next week's problem-solving tasks, reflected on what was working and not working with specific students, and identified strategies to better engage those students having difficulty. They then created a portfolio of student work in each classroom. At the end the quarter, they used the portfolio as the base for assessing what worked in this pilot, what they would do differently when they used the instrument again, and what help they needed from their consultant-mentor.

Phase 2: Making Sense of the Data

The second learning phase in the pilot stage involved teachers in an analysis of the data gathered. The teachers worked to understand their innovation in relation to their students' needs, assess its implications and ramifications, and analyze the introduction tasks. After this discussion, the teachers developed their individual lesson plans based on what they understood about the innovation and their students' needs from this data.

Phase 3: Transfer of Understanding

In the third learning phase, transfer, the teachers used what they had planned, met to discuss the results and gathered evidence about the degree of success. The school's professional developer provided a consultant to meet once a month with each team, observe in classrooms, conference with individual teachers, and give feedback to the principal and professional developer (see an example of such visits in Figure 6.3). At the conclusion, the teachers in grade-level teams reviewed the assessment data that they were using to track student progress to make a judgment on the pilot's transfer of understanding.

Figure 6.3   The Pencil Story: A Mentor Overcomes Doubts

When I walked into the classroom, my heart sank. I had prepared to see the children working with the first instruments "organization of dots." On a shelf next to the teacher's desk, the pages were piled in neat folders, untouched.

"I am disappointed," I said to the teacher. "I thought this was the time the students would be working on these instruments."

"They can't do it," the teacher responded.

"Why do you think that?" I asked.

"They can't hold the pencils. Three-year-olds are not developmentally ready. Our Head-Start handbook tells us that."

"Do you mind if I try?"

"No. Go right ahead, but if they can't hold the pencil, they can't connect the first dots."

I sat down next to a three-year-old Inuit boy. He smiled at me, but did not pick up the pencil I offered to him. After I talked with him and told him who I was, I drew three sets of two dots on a large sheet of newsprint.

"What do you see in this picture," I asked as I pointed to the dots.

"Spots."

"How many?" I asked as I framed the first set.

"One.....Two," he said as he pointed to each dot.

"Very good."

I smiled as I emphasized the "very."

I continued, "Do you think I can draw a box around them?"

"Yes."

I drew the lines carefully around the pair. "Now, if I show you how to hold the pencil, do you think you could box the two dots right on top of my line?"

"Yes," he beamed.

I set the pencil between my fingers and thumb.

"Look how I am holding the pencil. This is what I want you to do. Okay?"

"Yes."

I gave him the pencil. I adjusted his fingers.

"Squeeze."

(Continued)

Figure 6.3 (Continued)

He squeezed. Slowly and precisely, I guided his hand to make the box.
"Perfecto!" I explained. "You did it. Now, do you think you can pick out two
more dots so we can draw a box? "
    "Yes," he said as he bent his head to the task. He pointed to the next pair he saw.
    "Bravo!" I explained in my most excited voice. With a large grin, I clapped my
hands. "You did it. Now, do you think you could draw a box around these two dots?"
    I then showed his successful work to the other students. I encouraged them to
give their classmate a round of applause. Then, I asked them, "How many of you
would like to try?" For the next twenty minutes, the teacher and I helped each of the
children grasp a pencil and draw boxes around matched pairs that they selected.
    Later that day, I asked the teacher, "What did you learn?"
    "I discovered that I was underestimating my children. With a little mediation,
they saw how to hold the pencils. I was amazed," she said.
    "Anything else?" I asked.
    "Yes. I saw how you mediated their precision and helped them make the lines
straight and the corners sharp. You gave them two new words, 'precise and
accurate.' It was very hands-on as they started to use the words to describe how
careful they had to be."
    "How about the math? Did they learn anything?" I asked.
    "Yes. I think so. After they were all finished with the big sheet, you gave them
the small sheet. You gave them the word 'square' and helped them find square in
the sets. You also gave them the words 'set' and 'pairs. ' When you were finished,
you checked to see how many could pick out 'sets' and 'pairs.' It opened my eyes
to what they could do with careful mediation. I had doubted that they could
even hold the pencil. Now, I see how much more they can do that I never
thought was possible."

LESSONS LEARNED: THE VALUE OF COACHING FOR TRANSFER

This teacher's final summary demonstrated the power and the importance of follow-up: coaching for transfer. Here was a teacher who had expressed her excitement after she had completed the initial "workshop" in Phase 1. Her information-gathering experience had a mix of new theory, demonstration, and guided practice. Soon after, she had participated in Phase 2 discussions. With her colleagues, she worked to make sense of the new ideas swarming in her head. She analyzed the concepts and practices learned; reflected on the values, drawbacks and benefits as related to her students; and planned how she would use what she learned in her daily schedule. She ended this learning phase, while preparing how she and her team would assess the project's impact on the identified student needs.

Back in the classroom, a glitch occurred. Instead of starting Phase 3 by initiating the first lessons, her doubts overcame her excitement and she let her plan sit. She took the materials that the district had provided for implementing the program and put them on a book shelf. As is often the case, even with less complex tasks than called for in the story relayed in the pencil story, the instruments may have remained forever on the shelf without the strong intervention of the mentor-coach.

As soon as the teacher's mentor crossed the classroom's threshold, the mentor made a quick assessment. Based on observations of the teacher's response to her questions, the mentor knew what steps she would recommend for the teacher to take. The mentor intervened, mediated the problem by showing the teacher how to overcome the pencil "excuse" and get students engaged. From there, the mentor prompted the students to label with the words "precise," "accurate," "set," and "pair" first by stating the words and then by asking the students to use the words as they counted the dots in each set.

The mentor's coaching ended when she asked the teacher to summarize what she had learned. The mentor wanted the teacher not only to explain how her doubts about the students' ability to hold the pencils were overcome, but also to articulate what other learning was made possible for the students once this obstacle was removed. In this way, when the teacher prepared the next lesson, she could use what she had discovered about her students capabilities to move to the next step.

The next step would then start with three figures. This step would give her the chance to mediate the students in distinguishing sets of two versus sets of three, while being precise and accurate in drawing lines, counting, drawing sets, and labeling sets. Following the coach's modeling in this first experience, the teacher would be encouraged to guide the students' task again with slightly more complex sets while continuing to emphasize the cognitive functions of precision, accuracy, labeling, and distinguishing.

"Whose bright idea was it to buy these in the first place?"

The interaction depicted in the pencil story spotlights common occurrences that can happen after teachers prepare their use of new concepts and practices. How many districts have provided teachers with classroom computers, a quick inservice, and the expectation that the teachers would move their students into the electronic learning world, only to discover that the computers sat unboxed in a closet? How often do schools provide workshops for teachers in thinking skills, multiple intelligences, or cooperative learning only to see the most superficial applications on a regular basis? After an initial burst of energy, the new strategies are labeled "unworkable" and allowed to fade. How many saw no applications of new ideas developed through expensive workshops that lacked the necessary coaching support and follow-up?

Once teachers know or select the content of their professional development program for the pilot innovation, the professional developer can introduce the components of the program that will best enable the teachers to try out what they learned on a regular schedule. The first phase of this innovative stage will involve teachers' *gathering information* about the innovation. They may participate in a workshop with a stimulating instructor, do team action research with print or online materials, complete a group investigation, or take graduate courses to address the key learning needs of their students. All can read the same material, or the group members individually can jigsaw the information-gathering task.

In whatever configuration (individual, small group, or total team) or analysis process that the teachers use in the second phase of learning, they *make sense* of the information they gathered. This essentially requires them to analyze the information in the light of the identified learning needs. They decipher what part of the information may make the best match to enable them to change the learning habits of their students. Do they concentrate on basic comprehension skills? How will a plan that includes using graphic organizers help with comprehension, thinking, and students' beliefs work? Can any of the software programs they reviewed help?

The innovation stage is completed only after the initiation of the third phase of learning. In this phase, teachers *put their application plans to work*. Very often, it is necessary that the plans include opportunities to peer coach, work with a mentor or consultant coach, or continue study in a support group. Especially in the early weeks and months, the support and guidance of a second party provides the benefit of pushing novice implementers through the first barriers to implementation. This support also speeds the teachers' refinement of their new challenge and encourages deeper reflection about what they are seeing in this first stage innovation. Figure 6.4 provides a quick checklist for each phase.

Figure 6.4   A Checklist for Piloting an Innovative Idea

> ❑ Invite coach to observe, give feedback, and guide reflection.
> ❑ Follow pilot application schedule.
> ❑ Observe student reactions and collect artifacts.
> ❑ Discuss results in peer teams.
> ❑ Modify innovations to fit student needs.

Joyce and Showers' landmark study (1983) spotlighted the glaring weakness of professional development programs that did little more than treat practicing teachers who were overwhelmed with the challenges of low performing students with quick fixes and band aides. "Here," these programs said, "is the information on how to increase achievement. Go forth and do." In essence, this study showed how teachers, like other professionals in other fields, benefited from the support of coaching as they tried better ways to teach. Sadly, the information-dumping model still dominates too many professional development efforts.

SUMMARY POINTS

1. There are three stages in a change project supported by professional development. In this first stage, teachers are engaged in a three-*phase* learning process that promotes transfer of learning from information gathered to information applied and tested.

2. The first stage ends when the teachers implement their knowledge in the classroom at least as a pilot test for them to assess. This successful transfer is the first major sign of the change process in action.

3. Coaching, in any of its forms, provides the principle and most necessary support method for encouraging the transfer of learning into each classroom. Whether in a preschool or a community college, professional development that just dumps information about a better way to help students learn has less than a 10 percent chance of making change (Joyce & Showers, 1983).

A Reality Check

Innovation means taking impossible ideas and turning them into reality.

—John Edwards

"This too will pass," the first teacher said.

"No doubt," said the second. "Every year they give us a fad for the future. Easy come, easy go."

"I can do a whole list: 'Hunter's seven steps to heaven.' 'Cooperative learning, multiple intelligences.' 'Standards.' The list goes on."

"That's why I can predict this latest thing will pass. I can just go back in my room and shut the door."

"Too bad," chimed in the third teacher, "that we never got to study any of them well. We get an edutainer the first week of school, lots of rah-rah and then it is 'Go and do.'"

"Do nothing, you mean."

"For once, I wish the powers that be would at least stick with one idea for a year or two."

In many schools, cynicism about professional development dominates the faculty's conversation. Best practices labeled as professional development establish the "Ho-hum. What else is new?" attitude. Fortunately, this can be remedied, and the best cure starts with the first dose of medicine: the student-centered needs assessment. When the results of this data are analyzed and used to plan innovative changes in instruction, the school is starting to march down a road that will change teachers' attitudes and lead to examining the innovations for the possibility of their sustainability. While encouraging, this is still challenging, and even after a year of success with the innovation, the path will stay rocky.

Teachers who have suffered the slings and arrows of poor professional development should remain cynical until they see the "proof in the pudding." Effective professional developers can lead this change by insisting on sufficient time and resources to refine the innovation. This begins with the opportunity to collaborate with site administrators in the search for sustainability.

A New Beginning for a New Way

When school leaders and their professional development specialists plan efforts that will lead to changing what teachers know and do by helping them transfer innovations into the classroom, they must consider not only the effort to pilot the change in daily practice, but also how teachers will *sustain* the innovations over many years. Because of the many pressures that can distract the teachers in any school day, it is important that the professional developer maintain a leadership role in keeping the focus on the change effort. This begins a concentrated effort to refine those first stage practices judged "promising for us" or "successful." Stage 2, then, is the important refinement stage.

Because positive gains in student achievement with higher test scores in mathematics, reading, writing, and other subjects are usually meant to last longer than one year, professional developers need to build into each effort a way to develop the project's sustainability. They have to "keep the energy flowing." When the professional development program is planned for a multiyear, multistage implementation, teachers will need time and support to refine the implementation. Teachers will need the time not only to assess the results shown by standardized tests, but also time to assess the implementation process and then build structures that will increase the chances of a long-term, sustainable program. Most importantly, teachers will have the opportunity to allow for novice "mistakes" and take both pride and increased ownership of the change process itself by being allowed the chance to refine what they have started.

STAGE 2: THE REFINEMENT YEAR

In Stage 2, refinement, the professional developer forms a project leadership team. This team—led by the principal, facilitated by the professional developer or an external consultant, and including grade-level representatives—will assess what and how teachers, who are grouped in implementation teams, function as they turn the Stage 1 pilot into a more permanent feature of the school's response to student needs. This leadership team should meet at least once per month over the next school year to focus on the refinement stage.

In this stage, what the now-seasoned innovators want to know is "what is working?" "What needs refining?" and "Where do we need help?" (See Figure 7.1.) A school portfolio can be a key means to answering these questions. With student data from student test scores, teachers' own observations and analyses, artifact analysis, and external feedback portfolio, the teachers can track the project's progress as it moves through Stage 2.

During this stage, it is counterproductive for the district, site leader, or professional developers to distract the teachers with other professional development activities. No professional conferences. No district inservice requests. No edutainers on

Figure 7.1   Assessing Program Progress

- What are we doing well with this pilot?
- What can we do differently to improve or refine the project?
- What help do we need?

district institute days. Unless such activities contribute directly to the project, the site leadership team needs to keep the staff on focus with the principal project.

Phase 1: Gathering Information to Decide the Future

When the school community decides to move to Stage 2 in order to refine the program, it is ready to begin fine-tuning of the project. In this stage, teachers adapt the program's delivery to their students' needs and their own teaching styles. There are six elements that require consideration:

- goals and measurable outcomes
- tactical checklists
- investigation questions
- team configurations
- assessment strategies and tools
- reporting processes

Goals and Measurable Outcomes

What attribute best marks a collaborative, schoolwide effort? Johnson and Johnson (1986) answer this question by espousing "a common or shared goal" as the key to success of any collaborative group. This shared goal, however, must go beyond mere "espousal." It needs delineation with outcomes that members of the learning community will continually review. Data must also be gathered to measure their collaborative effort.

The community will focus on this common goal by aligning all outcomes and professional development activities in the project. Are these outcomes:

1. Responsive to the learners' needs, especially for the lowest performing students?

2. Measurable by attainable data?

3. Able to sustain commitment to the project?

The target graphic in Figure 7.2 provides a representation of a school that puts the learner's needs at the center. All activity spirals outward from that center. Goals and outcomes form the next rings, followed by professional development activities and the data each activity generates.

Figure 7.2   Targeting Learner Needs Over Time

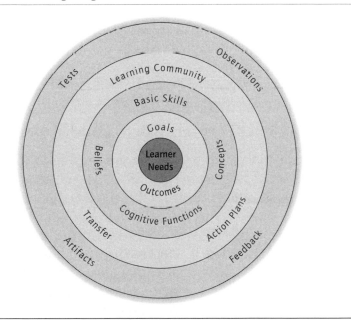

Tactical Checklists

The checklist tactic was first developed by test pilots in 1935. Boeing aircraft had just won the contract to build the new B-17, the flying fortress. Its control system for takeoffs was so far advanced that the best test pilots could not recall all the procedures. Several takeoffs had ended in crashes. The test pilots then put their heads together and came up with the checklist solution. Today, on all planes, including the most advanced super-jumbos, pilots and copilots use this method before each flight.

More recently, intensive care units in hospitals have adopted the checklist. In December 2006, the *New England Journal of Medicine* reported that the infection rate in Michigan Intensive Care Units decreased by 66 percent. Some hospitals reduced infection rates to 0 percent saving more than 1500 lives. "The successes," wrote Atwal Gawande in his *New Yorker* article, "have been sustained for almost four years—all because of a stupid little checklist" (2007, p. 94).

Likewise, peer coaching can use the three key components of the checklist procedure borrowed from the air and medical models:

1. Teams construct their own tactical checklists, which are reviewed by their mentor coaches.

2. Team members observe each other with the lists in hand.

3. Individuals in each team share the results and highlight omissions only with each other. The observations and the post conferences are confidential and nonevaluative.

Using the steps above, teachers start using tactical checklists in peer support teams. Working together, they construct a checklist for a tactic such as the "think-pair-share" (see Figure 7.3). In the first trials, one team member prepares use of the tactic with the checklist in hand. When that team member uses the checklist during a lesson, a second team member observes with the checklist in hand. During the lesson, the observer may signal if a component is missed, or the observer may wait for a post classroom conference to provide the feedback. The team members work with each other and the checklist until each feels comfortably in command when using the tactic.

Figure 7.3   Think-Pair-Share: A Tactical Checklist

- ❑ Introduce the tactic.
- ❑ Demonstrate each signal with instructions for student action.
- ❑ Present question with think instruction.
- ❑ Wait.
- ❑ Present pair instruction.
- ❑ Wait: monitor without interrupting.
- ❑ Present all class-sharing instruction.
- ❑ Review pass and no duplication guidelines.
- ❑ Draw names from a hat to share.
- ❑ Use web on board to record each new idea.
- ❑ Call for a student summary.
- ❑ Recognize student thinking.

Instructional Investigation

The "instructional investigation" is a strategy for facilitating teachers' searches for best ways to solve persistent instructional problems. Instructional investigations are apt strategies for solving the mystery of plateaued academic performances.

There are two types of questions that guide instructional investigations. The first is the *launch* question; second are the *mediation-probes*.

The launch question, always built on the priority learning needs of the targeted low performing students, initiates a long-term professional development process that is intended to result in measurable student changes via the transfer of teacher learning to the classroom. The launch question defines teachers as application researchers. The teachers will take advantage of primary research—usually done in a controlled university-based study—about learning theory, best practices, student populations, cultures, and factors studied in highly controlled situations and guided by criteria for scientifically based research. The primary research will seed the teachers' application studies (see Figure 7.4 for examples).

Figure 7.4   From Scientifically Based Research to Application
Research in the Classroom: An Example

Mary Budd Rowe (1972), in work funded by the National Science Foundation (NSF), studied the effects of teacher "wait time" on student achievement. A second project, Teacher Expectations and Student Achievement (Kerman, 1979) embedded "wait time" tactics in its list of instructional tactics that increased student achievement. With the help of Phi Delta Kappa, T. L. Good (1987) and his colleagues also researched the impact of wait-time on student achievement. Over the years, teachers in the Los Angeles and other school districts applied wait time and other tactics in their classrooms. Many conducted follow-up action research projects that studied their own use of the tactics.

In their projects, teachers cannot be expected to have the resources and time to conduct the purer forms of primary research. Instruction, not research, is their "business." However, teachers can use the results of primary studies to launch their own investigations, as have many teachers with such strategies as question asking, summarizing, comparing, and hypothesizing (Marzano et al., 2001). These site-based studies are intended to provide each school with the information needed to determine what best practices will be most beneficial for its students.

Strong launch questions not only raise hypothetical questions about the possible impact of a proven strategy for addressing the needs of a school's students, they are structured to provide the data that will help the teachers decide what strategies work best, make changes, and refine the school's instructional practices. Thus, strong launch questions lead to measurable numbers.

As illustrated in Figure 7.5, launch questions need not meet the "golden standard" applied to primary research. Yes, it is nice when application projects can have control and experimental groups as well the pre- and post testing as called for by primary research. However, such a standard is not practical in most school-based application projects.

Figure 7.5   Sample Launch Questions

Basic Skills: How can we improve seventh grade Hispanic students' reading comprehension scores in language arts, mathematics, and social studies by at least 7 percent per year over the next three years?

Cognitive Functions: How can we reduce our third grade students' impulsive classroom responses during guided instruction in science by 15 percent over the next three years?

Belief Systems: What best practice strategies will best enable at least 90 percent of our African American freshmen and sophomores apply to colleges?

Probe Questions

From a practical perspective, launch questions help teachers ask additional questions, or *probe questions,* which will allow them to dig more deeply into what is happening with their students' performance. These probe questions allow the teachers to use multiple sources of information which encourage them to think more deeply about how they approach instruction with the targeted students (see Figure 7.6). Their observations are based on performance rubrics they construct, checklists of what students do and say in response to various instructional strategies, and comparative analysis of students' artifacts including writing samples, lab exercises, and classroom comments. All of these observations provide important data that allows more accurate information and clearer responses to the launch questions.

Figure 7.6   Sample Probe Questions

---

1. How does our data on the third grade students compare to national norms?
2. What more specific outcomes will identify the additional reading skills that our students must develop?
3. Which of the cognitive functions are most deficient in our students?

Team Configurations

In a developing learning community, small team collaboration is an essential ingredient. This small team collaboration improves communication, deepens commitment, and enables two to three staff members to bond more rapidly. In a project, the professional development specialist for the site has the responsibility to coordinate the teams and facilitate the development of team unity within the learning community. And, many small collaborations bond the larger community collaboration.

When well-coordinated, application teams may be the most sure-footed and speediest pathway to a learning community that is positively interdependent, unified by a shared goal, and individually accountable (Johnson & Johnson, 1986). Such teams come in a variety of forms and configurations:

- *Cross-disciplinary teams.* These teams are especially useful in middle and secondary schools when the focus is on the need to dramatically improve basic skills, cognitive functions, or students' own beliefs about learning potential. For the improvement of basic skills, the teams focus on helping all staff become teachers of reading, math, or writing. Teams design and track best practices within content areas to incorporate the basic skills into the various subjects on a regular basis. When addressing the issue of negative student beliefs, these teams are especially valuable. The cross-disciplinary nature of the teams allow teachers to discuss the issues and strategies from their multiple perspectives.

- *Base groups.* These teams are especially useful in elementary schools. Like cross-disciplinary teams, three to five teachers meet on alternate weeks for one class period. They set and review the project goals; share student artifacts that show samples of good, satisfactory, and unsatisfactory student work related to the goals; analyze test data; and discuss individual student progress. Most importantly, they share ideas for helping the most struggling students.

- *Peer support teams.* These teams consist of two to three teachers from the same grade level and/or content area. They meet at least twice a month for one class period. Each member's principle responsibility is to provide the other members support as they "try out" their action plans. After reviewing their goal, they develop a tactical list that will guide the mutual observations of the plan's implementation in each classroom. This helps the team prepare each strategy with a detailed task analysis. During the observation, all team members follow the list. The observer checks off items. Sometimes, the observer may signal the teacher if an item is missed. After the observation, the peers meet to review the list and make suggestions. See Figure 7.3 on page 85.

- *Departmental teams.* These teams include all members of the department. Each department determines the size of any subgroups. If subgroups are aligned by course or grade, they often employ the jigsaw. In the jigsaw, each member of a group takes a part of the task. At the end of each quarter, the subgroups meet with the entire department team to share the impact on student learning and the value of the tactics they have developed.

- *Grade-level teams.* Elementary teachers meet as teams with their grade-level peers. An effective tactic for these teams is the group investigation (Sharon & Sharon, 1992). The teachers agree on a launch question related to the students' learning needs. For instance, a team might ask "How do we help our students with special needs reduce their impulsivity and become more reflective without negatively affecting the other students?" The teachers agree to research the question using the jigsaw technique. Each teacher will read a different article related to the question and interview the author via e-mail. Teachers will then summarize their findings and present them to the team. After agreeing on the best solution(s), they will construct an action research project with their students. They will base the project on their launch question and allow time for each teacher to gather data for the all-group discussion of results.

- *Site leadership team.* This team, lead by the principal, coordinates communication among the other teams in the site's project. The principal can ask the professional development specialist, a supervisor, or a teacher to facilitate. However, it is essential that the principal head the effort and communicate enthusiasm and commitment for the professional development.

   The leadership team will consist of the principal plus a representative from each team. The representative rotates each year. This representative can be the union site representative or others that the principal might select such as subject area consultants or specialists (e.g., reading, math), department chairs, or grade-level team leaders. This team should meet at least once per month to review the project plan, identify systemic obstacles, resolve those issues that are site based, and pass those that are district based to the district professional development team. It helps if the principal facilitates these meetings using a standard format (see Figure 7.7) that is kept in the project's portfolio.

Figure 7.7   Sample Monthly Review Format

Project Plan Monthly Review

Team: _____ Date: _____

Project Title: _____

Project Goal:

Obstacles to Discuss:
  1.
  2.
  3.

Strategy per Obstacle   Person Responsible   Completion Date
  1.
  2.
  3.

Other Items:

Phase 2: Making Continuous Assessments

Assessment *cycles* through Stage 2 (see Figure 7.8). This means that assessment is not just done at the end of the project. Each month, as teachers review the students' progress as impacted by the project's strategies and tactics, they gather data that informs instructional decisions. The cycle encourages teacher teams to analyze information on an ongoing basis. As they gather the data and determine what modifications they will make to improve use of the strategies and tactics, they cycle these into their new lesson plans on an ongoing basis. Then, once again, they gather data to determine how successful they are in meeting the students' learning needs. This cyclical approach informs the teachers how well students are responding to the strategies, tactics, and programs they are continuing to refine.

Figure 7.8   Assessment Cycles Through Stage 2

The Phases of the Refinement Stage

1. *Gathering Information*

2. *Making Continuous Assessments*

3. *Implementing Refinements*

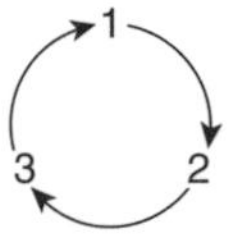

Timing

Teams establish the amount of time they will spend on assessment. Assessment meetings should occur at least monthly and allow time for thorough discussion of the data before new plans are made.

Meeting Content

Peer teams or individuals report the data results gathered from the classroom to the group. A recorder collects the data and posts it on an overhead, blackboard, newsprint, or projector for all to see. A facilitator then guides the data analysis in search of positive and negative patterns. Following the analysis, the facilitator will guide the discussion of refinements to make.

Eligible Data Formats

The group determines what data formats members will use. These may include artifacts of student work, teacher observation checklists, teacher-made quizzes and test results, rubrics, etc. (see rubric example in Figure 7.9). In order to keep analysis simple, it is important that the team agrees on which format(s) all will use.

Phase 3: Implementing Refinements and Reporting Results

Each time the team's data shows a need to refine the project (rather than "throw the baby out with the bathwater" or dismiss

Figure 7.9   A Sample Rubric: Cognitive Functions

Precision in Fourth Grade Math

To what degree do my students:

1. Perform operations with attention to exact numbers?

   /———————————————/———————————————/
   always   sometimes   never

2. Copy material without mistakes?

   /———————————————/———————————————/
   always   sometimes   never

3. Include all key information when describing problems?

   /———————————————/———————————————/
   always   sometimes   never

4. Perform problems according to instructions?

   /———————————————/———————————————/
   always   sometimes   never

5. Include correct signs?

   /———————————————/———————————————/
   always   sometimes   never

---

as "it doesn't work"), the members adjust their instructional strategies. After analyzing the data, the team has three questions to answer:

1. What does the data say we are doing well?

2. What do we need to do differently?

3. What help do we need?

This review is especially important when one or more teachers is having difficulty with the implementation. The first question helps the team recognize what facet of a strategy is working. It tells the members that "this is what *we* are doing successfully to impact our students' learning." If the school has experienced a large amount of poor student performance over several years, this self-recognition is extremely important in helping teachers see the power of their professional contributions and its correlation with student success.

The second question avoids the "blame game" and prevents "doubting Thomases" from taking some element of the innovation that is not going well and using it to bash the entire effort. It is also the question that provides the fodder for making refinements to the project so that it fits more closely to the students of "this" school. The question says to the teachers: "You are the experts on your students. What do we need to do more precisely and exactly so that the strategy or program works better for them?"

The third question encourages the team to identify issues and barriers that its members don't have the knowledge or skills to resolve. They may need to call upon the professional development specialist for help in analyzing data or finding an expert who can help with interpreting a standard or understanding a concept. Or, it may call for a series of hands-on sessions that give the teachers more expertise in using some of the strategies that they have identified as important.

SUMMARY POINTS

1. In Stage 2, site leadership teams review Stage 1 results and decide on continuation or cancellation.

2. Teams that move to Stage 2 develop and implement a refinement plan that enables teachers to tailor the program to their classrooms on an ongoing basis throughout the year.

3. Data gathering, analysis, and application become key tools for Stage 2 refinements.

The
Sustainability
Factor

To the Okanagen people . . . the realization that the total community must be engaged in order to attain sustainability comes as a result of surviving together for thousands of years.

—Center for Ecoliteracy

The first question took Melissa by surprise. She had just presented an example of a school improvement project that had produced phenomenal results. Its effect size, after only two years, was in the high 60s. "If it was so successful," the questioner asked, "why did it die off?"

Melissa took a moment to gather her thoughts. "That is a really good question," she started. "I hadn't thought much about it. Off the top of my head, I would say the first was financial. The

(Continued)

(Continued)

district was hit with multimillion-dollar cuts. Most of the professional development went."

"But couldn't the teachers continue on their own?"

"Some did," Melissa said. "But those were the ones who saved their materials. There was no money for the new teachers. And, the district had a large turnover. I guess the real reason was that we never really thought about sustaining it. The end came so fast. We had never discussed what it would take to have the project survive."

After two or three years of assessment and refinement of a professional development program geared for change, it is appropriate for the learning community to decide the long-term fate of the project. This is the third stage.

Does the community believe the improvements in instruction should become a permanent part of the school culture? Should teachers continue to modify and refine what they are doing? Should they trash the innovation and go a different direction? Is the innovation worth sustaining? Should they weave it into the fabric of the school's culture?

At this point, the site leadership team is "in charge" of the project. The professional developer assists in the support roles of coordinator, climate controller, creative problem solver, and coach. However, it is essential to a project going into this third stage that all understand that the successful long-term survival of the project depends not on any one individual or team. The project's sustainability is the responsibility of all in the learning community.

STAGE 3: PLANNING FOR SUSTAINABILITY

The major goal will focus the learning community on making the project an integral part of its *modus operandi* for the long term. To accomplish this goal, the community must formalize the project's structures, processes, and procedures within the school's institutional framework so that the project sustains the changes over time. In this process, the team integrates the new with the established (see Figure 8.1).

Figure 8.1   Sustaining New in the Old

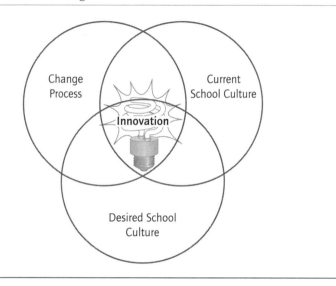

Sustaining Change for the Long Term

What will the leadership team do to ensure that they sustain an innovation? Professional developers or community members can create a checklist or fashion a rubric for sustaining the effort.

1. Recognize that sustainability of an innovation requires a *plan* of action. The plan will contain a collaborative goal, measurable outcomes, aligned professional development strategies and tactics, assessment tools, and timelines with assignment of tasks for integrating the innovation and the school's established culture.

2. Assign a team member to facilitate the project. This person is responsible for the annual team schedule, logistics, and other tools teachers will need to keep the project alive as they integrate the innovation into the daily schedule. They may rotate this position.

3. Identify and solidify professional development activities, which ensure that new teachers learn what they need to know for integrating the project into the school day.

4. Provide continuing professional development for experienced veterans of the project so that they can maintain a fresh outlook over time. Develop and encourage teacher leadership of the project.

5. Set up a library of professional materials that will keep all staff informed about new data related to the project. Include a bulletin board that encourages teachers to report on new project-related developments.

6. Provide teaching aides related to the project for teachers to post in their classrooms.

7. Conduct semiannual sharing sessions so that teachers can discuss new ideas related to the project, share student artifacts, and brainstorm new ideas.

8. Include assessments of teachers' use of the new instructional strategies in annual teacher goal setting and reviews.

9. Post annual student performance data to communicate ongoing successes from the project.

10. Invite teachers to write articles about their students in the parent newsletter.

11. Give an annual award to the teacher who demonstrated most improved use of the professional development received each year.

12. Rotate site leadership team's membership, one person per year. Schedule the team to meet twice annually to assess continued impact and needs for refinement.

13. Create a rubric for an annual assessment of how the community is faring with the new project.

14. Create a climate of fun and interest with novel ways for teachers to renew their spirit and commitment to the project. Make a plan each year to attend to this factor.

15. Encourage teachers to speak up and out. Arrange for them to present the program at professional conferences or to community groups.

Sustainability: The Professional Developer's Role

Figure 8.2   Sustainability

Sustainability is a characteristic of a process that can be maintained at an acceptable level indefinitely. The word is most usually associated with climate and other ecological changes, but is also being used in discussions of systemic stability maintenance in business, education, and industry.

The ultimate responsibility for sustaining a project falls on the shoulders of the site leadership team. The professional developer, however, can collaborate with the team in a variety of ways to support the leaders:

- *Coordinator of activities.* Ensures that all new professional development activities for this project align with the goals and outcomes for continuous improvement. Maintains a master schedule for developing new teachers, mentoring veteran teachers, gathering continuous assessment data, and holding team meetings.
- *Controller of climate.* Consults with the site leadership team on issues related to a climate that supports learning transfer so that the professional development activities continue to result in a high degree of student achievement.
- *Creative problem solver.* When glitches or barriers arise that interfere with the learning transfer and school

change processes, the professional developer leads problem solving activities that result in refined solutions.
- *Coach of coaches.* The professional developer coaches the
  principal and the leadership team members in regards
  to their leadership roles and duties. In addition, professional developers prepare the new mentors who will
  assist the new teachers in learning about and using the
  project.

LEARNING ACTIVITIES
THAT PROMOTE SUSTAINABILITY

In the early days of school improvement during the 1970s
and 1980s, the federal government supported large change
projects that relied on significant professional development.
The funds usually lasted for three years. In the third year, the
school district was supposed to declare how it would continue the project on its own. For the most part, districts
dropped the program when they lost the funding. If anything survived, it was materials produced or bought for the
project and a few teachers who continued to use what they
had learned.

Nevertheless, more recent developments show that sustainability is possible. In New York City, the Lexington School
for the Deaf adopted Feuerstein's Instrumental Enrichment
Program almost two decades ago. Although they knew little
of the term "sustainability," the commitment of the school's
leaders to Feuerstein's theory and practices solidified the
project's use as a core element in school's instructional
approach. As the years progressed, they recognized the neces-
sity of intentional hard work to sustain the program. New
teachers arrived. The funding sources changed. The superintendent retired. In spite of these "setbacks," the teachers and
administrators have continued with the program.

What did they do, and what are they still doing, to maintain commitment and excitement after twenty-plus years?

1. They prepared the site administrators to prepare teachers to use the program. They designed a professional development effort that started with an intense new teacher-training program and which used the school's classrooms and teachers to demonstrate the program in action.

2. They created mentor teachers to coach the new teachers.

3. The administrators mentor veteran teachers.

4. The administrators include the best practices for using the program in annual classroom observations and conferences.

5. Grade-level teams meet on a regularly scheduled basis.

6. Parents are informed about the program and given a chance to observe it in action. A future program plan will allow parents to obtain training in the program for at home use.

7. The administration funded the continuous purchase of the program's classroom materials, teacher training materials, and new teacher preparation.

8. The school set up a "Mediated Learning Center" with books, studies, schedules, and study space.

9. Visuals posted in classrooms, hall bulletin boards, and other prominent spots around the school celebrate the project and prompt the new ideas. Teachers maintain a "brag board."

10. The site leadership team develops annual goals to help teachers maintain interest and enthusiasm for the project.

11. Teachers take the lead in presenting the program to other schools, conferences, and community groups. Groups are invited into the school to see teachers in action using the program.

12. The administration established a new position: "Director of Mediated Learning." The director provides professional development for the teachers in the school and for two other satellite schools that have adopted the program; oversees the budget, schedules, and other logistics; and manages the program with an annual plan.

13. There is an annual review and discussion of standardized test scores at the start of the school year.

14. Teachers are invited to write professional articles on the project with an emphasis on students' successes.

A single activity introduced as an isolated or random event adds little to the goal of sustainability. Instead, when an activity is used as a strategy to advance the goal of sustainability, it takes on a new power. As the Lexington example shows, multiple strategies aligned with the goal enrich the process of change and ensure that the project continues. The process is not laissez faire. It is a process that is facilitated and managed with great care by those who are committed to its advancement.

SPECIAL EVENTS TO PROMOTE SUSTAINABILITY

Schools such as Lexington, which have successfully sustained a program dependent on professional development, take extra steps with special events that promote sustainability. The following samples were culled from the practices of these schools.

End-of-Year Exhibitions

In May, the site leadership team schedules time for each team to make an exhibit, in a booth they construct, showing the work it has done with classroom photographs, videos, and student artifacts. Some add data charts tracking student progress, selected portfolio pages, and a simple brochure for guests to take away. Parents, district administrators, community members, and teachers from other schools file by the exhibits, stop to discuss how the group's work aligns with the learning community's goals, and gather ideas about sustaining a professional development effort.

End-of-Year Celebrations

As each school year closes, the site leadership team organizes a celebration. After reviewing portfolios from grade-level and other teams, it prepares a presentation of what the learning community has accomplished in sustaining the project and meeting the annual improvement goals. If standardized test results are available, they present them to the entire learning community. They may also feature other results. The celebration, held on an evening or weekend, may include spouses or other interested persons with a potluck dinner or progressive deserts.

Incentives to Keep Going Forward

In current practice, most incentives for continuing educa tion are based on the old paradigm of acquiring information. When a teacher or principal finishes a course, a certificate program, or a degree program, the district awards either a step-and-scale pay increase or recertification points. When an inservice day is completed, inservice points are given. Time spent plus an A or a B on a knowledge test are the major criteria for any award.

In contrast, in the learning transfer paradigm where sustainability is valued, incentives are given for completed *application* of course knowledge over the long term. Not until teachers use a new concept or skill in their classroom are step-and-scale, career-ladder, or recertification points awarded. Additional points are given in succeeding years to acknowledge a teacher's or a team's efforts in sustaining an innovation. At five- and ten-year points, plaques are awarded.

Critical Concept Focus

When sustaining a program over time, a preeminent challenge is maintaining focus on its critical concepts. As the inevitable and multiple distractions emerge throughout the school year, site team leaders facilitate the staff's ability to weed out ancillary information. Roger and David Johnson's (1986) identification of the five basic elements of cooperative learning—positive interaction, face-to-face interaction, individual accountability, interpersonal and small group skills, and group processing, along with Fogarty and Bellanca's (1991) BUILD attributes of cognitive instruction, are examples of this high-transfer identifying practice that supports attention to the core values and critical concepts of a project over time.

Application Projects

Beyond lesson designs that incorporate teachers' new ideas, senior team members can help novice members produce classroom curriculum projects. These may include classroom learning centers, problem-based learning units, interdisciplinary hands-on projects with student materials, study kits, or other applications of ideas garnered in their study. The grade-level teams may gather and duplicate these projects as tools for keeping the project over time by aligning these projects with the core values of the change program, and teachers stay focused on those values.

SUMMARY POINTS

1. Sustainability is an intentional, managed quality that requires close attention over time.

2. The professional developer's role shifts from direct involvement in facilitating a change process to the facilitation of the leadership team's efforts to sustain the project.

3. Although a new concept in education, sustainable practices are increasing as schools appreciate the value of managing successful projects for the long term.

A Professional Developer's Checklist for Change

This checklist will enable the individuals responsible for professional development at a school to construct and follow a plan that puts into practice the ideas of this book. Such a plan will serve as a roadmap. For detailed information on the stops along the way, leaders can establish study teams to research and create specific, transfer-rich strategies. These strategies can sustain as integral parts of the learning community's culture of constructive change for higher student achievement.

- ❏ Assess Learning Needs of Low Performing Students
  - ❏ Basic Skills
  - ❏ Core Curricular Concepts
  - ❏ Cognitive Deficiencies
  - ❏ Negative Beliefs About Learning Potential

- ❏ Set Schoolwide Targets for Improving Student Achievement
  - ❏ Improve Basic Skills
  - ❏ Develop Concept Understanding
  - ❏ Strengthen Cognitive Functions
  - ❏ Transform Beliefs

- ❏ Establish Working Teams and Programs
  - ❏ Site Leadership Team for Professional Development
  - ❏ Sustainable Professional Development Program
  - ❏ Teacher Teams by Department, Grade Level, etc.
  - ❏ Peer Coaching and Support Teams

- ❏ Build Learning Community
  - ❏ Coordination of Effort
  - ❏ Shared Goals
  - ❏ Managed Collaborative Process
  - ❏ Ongoing Assessment

- ❏ Promote Transfer of Learning
  - ❏ Plan Each Stage and Phase
  - ❏ Build in Expectations and Support for Transfer
  - ❏ Assess Impact of Transfer

- ❏ Focus on Sustainability
  - ❏ Long-Term Incentives
  - ❏ Multiple Sources of Data
  - ❏ Selectively Abandon

References

Barth, R., et al. (2005). *On common ground*. Bloomington, IN: Solution Tree.

Bellanca, J. (2007). *Graphic organizers*. Thousand Oaks, CA: Corwin Press.

Ben-Hur, M. (Ed.). (1994). *On Feuerstein's instrumental enrichment: A collection*. Palatine, IL: IRI/Skylight Publishing.

Burke, K., Fogarty, R., & Belgrad, S. (2007). *The portfolio connection* (2nd ed.). Thousand Oaks, CA: Corwin Press.

Caro-Bruce, C. (2007). *Creating equitable classrooms through action research*. Thousand Oaks, CA: Corwin Press.

Cohen, A. (1993). A new educational paradigm. *Phi Delta Kappan, June*, 791–795.

Copland, M., & Knapp, M. (2006). *Connecting leadership with learning*. Alexandria, VA: Association for Supervision and Curriculum Development.

Costa, A. L. (1991). *The school as a home for the mind*. Palatine, IL: IRI/Skylight Publishing.

Costa, A. L., Bellanca, J., & Fogarty, R. (Eds.). (1992). *If minds matter: A foreword to the future* (Vol. 2). Palatine, IL: IRI/Skylight Publishing.

Costa, A. L., & Garmston, R. (1985). Supervision for intelligent teaching. *Educational Leadership, February*, 70, 72–80.

De Bono, E. (1992). *Serious creativity*. New York: Harper Collins.

Deming, E. (1986). *Out of the crisis*. Cambridge, MA: MIT Center for Advanced Engineering Study.

Eaker, E., & DuFour, R. (1999). *Professional learning communities at work*. Bloomington, IN: Solution Tree.

Feuerstein, R. (2006). *Instrumental enrichment*. Jerusalem, Israel. ICELP Press.

Fine, C. with Raack, L. (1994). Professional development: Changing times. *Policy Briefs, Report, 4*, 2–6.

Fogarty, R. (1989). *From training to transfer: The role of creativity in the adult learner*. Doctoral dissertation, Loyola University of Chicago, IL.

Fogarty, R. (1994). *The mindful school: How to teach for metacognitive reflection.* Palatine, IL: IRI/Skylight Publishing.

Fogarty, R., & Bellanca, J. (2003). *Blueprints for achievement in the cooperative classroom* (3rd ed.). Thousand Oaks, CA: Corwin Press.

Fogarty, R., Perkins, D., & Barell, J. (1992). *The mindful school: How to teach for transfer.* Palatine, IL: IRI/Skylight Publishing.

Fogarty, R., & Peete, B. (2006). *From staff room to classroom.* Thousand Oaks, CA: Corwin Press.

Fuhrman, S. H. (1994). Challenges in systemic education reform. *CPRE Policy Briefs,* 1–7.

Fullan, M. G. (2005). *International handbook of educational change.* Heidlebert, Germany: Springer.

Fullan, M. G. (2006). *Learning places.* Thousand Oaks, CA: Corwin Press.

Fullan, M. G. (2007). *The new meaning of educational change.* New York: Teachers College Press.

Gardner, H. (1983). *Frames of mind: The theory of multiple intelligences.* New York: Basic Books.

Gardner, H., & Boix-Mansilla, V. (1994). Teaching for understanding: Within and across disciplines. *Educational Leadership, February,* 14–18.

Garmston, R., Linder, C., & Whitaker, J. (1993). Reflections of cognitive coaching. *Educational Leadership, October,* 57–61.

Garner, B. (2007). *Getting to got it: Helping struggling students learn how to learn.* Alexandria, VA: Association for Supervision and Curriculum Development.

Gawande, A. (2007, December 10). The successes. *The New Yorker.*

Good, T. L. (July-August, 1987). Two decades of research on teacher expectations. *Journal of Teacher Education.*

Goodlad, J. I. (1990, November). Better teachers for our nation's schools. *Phi Delta Kappan,* pp. 184–194.

Goodlad, J. I. (1994). *Educational renewal: Better teachers, better schools.* San Francisco: Jossey-Bass.

Goodlad, J. I. (1994). The national network for educational renewal. *Phi Delta Kappan, April,* 632–638.

Gordon, S. (2004). *Professional development for school improvement.* Boston: Allyn and Bacon.

Hitt, W. (1994). *The leader-manager.* Columbus, OH: Battelle Press.

Hoerr, T. (2005). *The art of school leadership.* Alexandria, VA: Association for Supervision and Curriculum Development.

Hord, S. M. (2003). *Learning together, leading together.* New York: Teachers College Press.

Hunter, M. (1984). Knowing, teaching, and supervising. In P. L. Hosford (Ed.), *Using what we know about teaching* (pp. 169–203).

Alexandria, VA: Association for Supervision and Curriculum Development.

Johnson, D. W. & Johnson, R. (1986). *Circles of learning: Cooperation in the classroom.* Alexandria, VA: Association for Supervision and Curriculum.

Joyce, B. R., & Showers, B. (1983). *Power in staff development through research and training.* Alexandria, VA: Association for Supervision and Curriculum Development.

Joyce, B. R., & Showers, B. (1988). *Student achievement through staff development.* New York: Longman.

Kerman, S. (1979). Teacher expectations and student achievement: "Why did you call on me? I didn't have my hand up!" *Phi Delta Kappan, June,* 716–718.

Killion, J. (2007). *Assessing impact.* Thousand Oaks, CA: Corwin Press.

Knowles, M. S. (1975). *Self-directed learning: A guide for learners and teachers.* New York: The Adult Education Co.

Knowles, M. S. (1983). Adults are not grown-up children as learners. *Community Services Catalyst, Fall,* 4–8.

Lieberman, A., & McLaughlin, M. W. (1992). Networks for educational change: Powerful and problematic. *Phi Delta Kappan, May,* 673–677.

Lindsey, D. (2005). *Culturally proficient coaching.* Thousand Oaks, CA: Corwin Press.

Little, J. W. (1993). Teacher professional development in a climate of educational reform. *Educational Evaluation and Policy Analysis, Summer,* 129–151.

Love, N., et al. (2007) *The data coach's guide to improving instruction.* Thousand Oaks, CA: Corwin Press.

Marzano, R. (2007). *The art and science of teaching.* Alexandria, VA: Association for Supervision and Curriculum Development.

Marzano, R., et al. (2001). *Classroom strategies that work.* Alexandria, VA: Association for Supervision and Curriculum Development.

McCombs, D. L. (1996). Alternative perspectives in motivation. In L. Baker et al. (Eds.), *Developing engaged readers in school and home communities.* Mahwah, NJ: Lawrence Erbaum.

McLaughlin, M. W. (1993). What matters most in teachers' workplace content? In J. W. Little & M. W. McLaughlin (Eds.), *Teachers work: Individuals, colleagues, and contexts* (pp. 79–103). New York: Teachers College Press.

McLaughlin, M. W. (2006) *Building school based teacher learning communities.* New York: Teachers College Press.

Murphy, C. (2004). *Whole faculty study groups.* Thousand Oaks, CA: Corwin Press.

Murphy, J. (2005). *Connecting teacher leadership and school improvement*. Thousand Oaks, CA: Corwin Press.

National Education Commission on Time and Learning. (1994). *Prisoners of time*. Washington, DC: U.S. Government Printing Office.

O'Day, J., & Smith, M. S. (1993). Systemic school reform and educational opportunity. In S. H. Fuhrman (Ed.), *Designing coherent education policy: Improving the system* (pp. 313–322). San Francisco: Jossey-Bass.

O'Shea, M. (2005) *From standards to success: A guide for school leaders*. Alexandria, VA: Association for Supervision and Curriculum Development.

Oxman, W. G., & Barell, J. (1983, April 11–15). *Reflective thinking in schools. A survey of teacher perceptions*. Paper presented at the 67th Annual Meeting of the American Educational Research Association, Montreal, Quebec.

Palincsar, A. S., & Brown, A. L. (1986, March). *Guided, cooperative learning and individual knowledge acquisition. (Technical Report No. 372)*. Cambridge, MA: Bolt, Beranek & Newman, and Urbana, IL: Illinois University, Center for the Study of Reading. (ERIC Document Reproduction Service No. ED 270 738)

Patterson, J., & Kelleher, P. (2003) Resilient school leaders. Alexandria, VA: Association for Supervision and Curriculum Development.

Piaget, J. (1972). *The psychology of intelligence*. Totowa, NJ: Littlefield Adams.

Presseisen, B. (2007). *Teaching for intelligence*. Thousand Oaks, CA: Corwin Press.

Raywid, M. A. (1993). Finding time for collaboration. *Educational Leadership, September*, 30–34.

Rowe, M. B. (1972). Wait time and rewards as instructional variables. Paper presented at the National Association of Research in Science Teaching, Chicago, IL.

Salomon, G., & Perkins, D. (1988). Teaching for transfer. *Educational Leadership, September*, 22–32.

Samson, S. B. (1990). *The predictable failure of educational reform: Can we change course before it's too late?* San Francisco: Jossey-Bass.

Schmuck, R. (2005). *Practical action research for change*. Thousand Oaks, CA: Corwin Press.

Senge, P. (1990). *The fifth discipline: The art and practice of the learning organization*. New York: Doubleday.

Sharon, Y., & Sharon, S. (1992). *Group investigation*, New York: Teacher's College Press.

Showers, B. (1984). *Transfer of training: The contribution of coaching*. Eugene, OR: Center for Educational Policy and Management.

Slavin, R. E. (1991). Synthesis of research on cooperative learning. *Educational Leadership, February*, 71–82.

Smith, M. S., & O'Day, J. (1991). Systemic school reform. In S. Fuhrman & B. Malen (Eds.), *The politics of curriculum and testing* (pp. 233–267). Bristol, PA: Falmer Press.

Taggert, G. (2005). *Promoting reflective thinking in teachers*. Thousand Oaks, CA: Corwin Press.

Thorndike, E. L. (1969). *Educational psychology*. New York: Arno Press.

Vilani, S. (2005). *Mentoring and induction programs that support new principals*. Thousand Oaks, CA: Corwin Press.

Vygotsky, L. S. (1978). *Mind in society: The development of higher psychological processes* (M. Cole, V. John-Steiner, S. Scribner, & E. Souberman, Eds.). Cambridge, MA: Harvard University Press.

Williams, J. R., & Kopp, W. L. (1994). Implementation of Instrumental Enrichment and cognitive modifiability in the Taunton public schools: A model for systemic implementation in U.S. schools. In M. Ben-Hur (Ed.), *On feuerstein's instrumental enrichment: A collection* (pp. 261–272). Palatine, IL: IRI/Skylight Publishing.

Williams, R. B. (1993). *More than 50 ways to build team consensus*. Palatine, IL: IRl/ Skylight Publishing.

Winograd, P., Turner, T., & McCall, A. (1990, November 27–December 1). *Influential teachers and receptive students*. Paper presented at the 40th Annual Meeting of the National Reading Conference, Miami, FL.

York-Barr, J. (2005). *Reflective practice to improve schools*. Thousand Oaks, CA: Corwin Press.